Microsoft®

Word 2010

Prentice Hall
is an imprint of

PEARSON

Harlow, England • London • New York • Boston • San Francisco • Toronto • Sydney • Singapore • Hong Kong
Tokyo • Seoul • Taipei • New Delhi • Cape Town • Madrid • Mexico City • Amsterdam • Munich • Paris • Milan

PEARSON EDUCATION LIMITED

Edinburgh Gate
Harlow CM20 2JE
Tel: +44 (0)1279 623623
Fax: +44 (0)1279 431059
Website: www.pearsoned.co.uk

First published in Great Britain in 2010

Pearson Education is not responsible for the content of third party internet sites.

ISBN: 978-0-273-73614-1

British Library Cataloguing-in-Publication Data
A catalogue record for this book is available from the British Library

Library of Congress Cataloging-in-Publication Data
A catalog record for this book is available from the Library of Congress

10 9 8 7 6 5 4 3 2 1
14 13 12 11 10

Designed by pentacorbig, High Wycombe

Typeset in 11/14 pt ITC Stone Sans by 30
Printed in Great Britain by Scotprint, Haddington.

Microsoft®
Word
2010

in Simple
steps

Robin Noelle

Use your computer with confidence

Get to grips with practical computing tasks with minimal time, fuss and bother.

In Simple Steps guides guarantee immediate results. They tell you everything you need to know on a specific application; from the most essential tasks to master, to every activity you'll want to accomplish, through to solving the most common problems you'll encounter.

Helpful features

To build your confidence and help you to get the most out of your computer, practical hints, tips and shortcuts feature on every page:

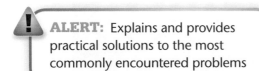 **ALERT:** Explains and provides practical solutions to the most commonly encountered problems

 **HOT TIP:** Time and effort saving shortcuts

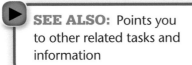 **SEE ALSO:** Points you to other related tasks and information

 **DID YOU KNOW?** Additional features to explore

WHAT DOES THIS MEAN?
Jargon and technical terms explained in plain English

Practical. Simple. Fast.

Acknowledgements:

I'd like to thank my agent, Neil Salkind at Studio B, for his continued support and Pearson Education for the opportunity to write this book. Special thanks to Chris Bryant at Microsoft for his assistance during this project. This book is for my dad who got me hooked on computers with that first TRS-80 and a Compuserve account. I love you and thanks for teaching me almost everything I know about technology.

Contents at a glance

Contents

Top 10 Word 2010 Tips

1 Getting to know Word

2 Customising with Word options

3 Creating basic Word documents

4 Advanced formatting for Word documents

5 Page layout and personalisation

6 Printing and mail merge

7 Graphics and photos

8 Using tables and charts

9 Lists and outlines

10 Language, research and spelling

11 Collaboration and co-authoring

12 Online collaboration and Office Live

13 Creating blogs and using web elements

Top 10 Word 2010 Problems Solved

Top 10 Word 2010 Tips

Tip 1: Create a new document using a template

The engineers who designed Word know that we aren't all designers at heart. To that end, they've created a plethora of templates that you can use to quickly create professional looking documents. With so many to choose from, both in Word and online, it's easy to find one that meets your needs.

1 Click File.

2 Click New.

3 Click a category folder in the Office.com Templates window.

4 Click a template to see more information and a preview.

5 Click Download to download the template and open it as a new document.

HOT TIP: Check out More Templates at the bottom of the screen. You'll have access to dozens more template categories.

DID YOU KNOW?

Any templates that you download and use will be stored in the Recent Templates folder. Look for them there when you want to access them again.

Tip 2: Apply a theme to your document

Applying a theme to your document gives it a professional and consistent look. The colours, fonts and styles have all been chosen for you. Using a theme gives you the benefits of using a professional designer without the cost.

1 Open your document.

2 Click Page Layout.

3 Click Themes.

4 Place your cursor over a theme to view its effects.

5 Click a theme to apply it.

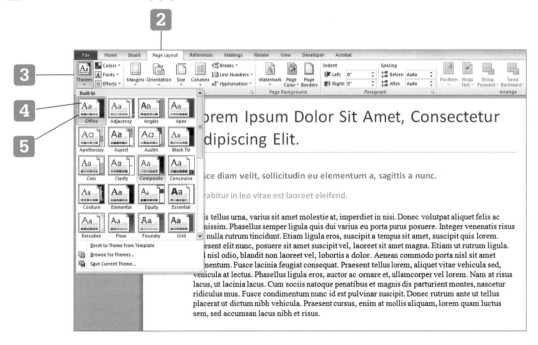

? DID YOU KNOW?

Applying a theme changes the styles that are used in your document. Click the Home tab and view the Styles box to see which style set your theme is using.

 HOT TIP: You can find more themes online. Download one and then select Browse for Themes to find a theme file on your computer, and then open it.

Tip 3: Save your document to be compatible with previous Word versions

When you have the most current version of Word, you can open many types of documents, including those created with an earlier version. However, if someone is running an older version of Word, they won't be able to open documents saved in the new Word file format. You can prevent this by saving your document in compatibility mode.

1 Click File.

2 Click Save As.

3 Click Save as Type to expand the menu.

4 Select Word 97-2003 as your file type.

5 Name your document and browse to your Save location.

6 Click Save to save your file.

HOT TIP: You can also save your document as a plain or rich text file. Plain text offers no formatting and rich text allows basic formatting like bold and italics.

DID YOU KNOW?

Maintaining compatibility with previous Word versions means that some of the elements in Word 2010 cannot be used. Text Effects, Word Art and other features will not work in older versions of Word.

Tip 4: Preview your document prior to printing

After you've carefully designed and crafted your document, you don't want any formatting surprises when you print it out. It's a good idea to preview what it will look like before you waste ink on printing something that's not quite right.

1 Click File.

2 Click Print.

3 Use the Zoom slider to zoom in and out of the preview.

4 Click Home to return to your document or Print to print it.

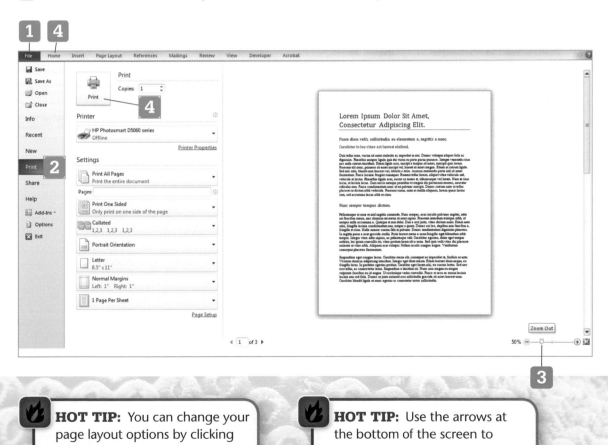

HOT TIP: You can change your page layout options by clicking Page Setup at the bottom of the Print window.

HOT TIP: Use the arrows at the bottom of the screen to flip through the pages of your document.

Tip 5: Use Find and Replace

The Find and Replace feature of Word 2010 can be an amazing time-saver when you need to use it. If you've misspelled or used an incorrect word in your text, this function will find all instances of that word and replace it with whatever you specify.

1 Click Home.

2 Click Replace in the Editing Group.

3 Type the word or phrase that you want to find in the Find what box.

4 Type the replacement word or phrase in the Replace with box.

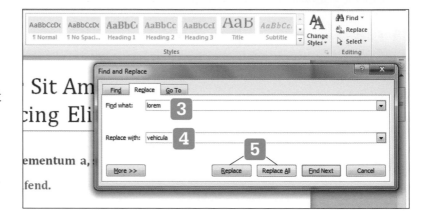

5 Click Replace to replace a single instance or Replace All to word search and replace all instances.

6 Review the results of the search and click OK to exit.

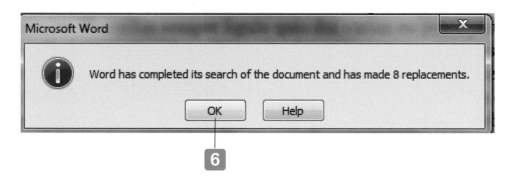

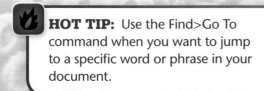

HOT TIP: Use the Find>Go To command when you want to jump to a specific word or phrase in your document.

HOT TIP: Click More in the Find and Replace dialogue box to see many more search options.

Tip 6: Use the Mini Toolbar to format text

Despite all the fun and creative tools available in Word 2010, what it really comes down to is manipulating text. The majority of the features that you'll use in Word will probably revolve around text formatting and fonts.

1 Select some text with your cursor.

2 Place your cursor over the Mini Toolbar that appears above the highlighted text to access it.

3 Select your font formatting changes.

4 Click anywhere in your document to close the Mini Toolbar.

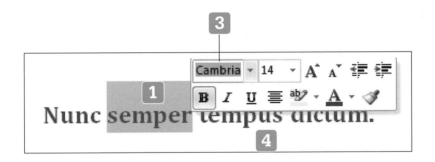

 HOT TIP: If you don't see the Mini Toolbar right away, move your cursor towards the upper right side of the highlighted text to find it.

? DID YOU KNOW?

You can use the Mini Toolbar to perform most of the functions usually found in the Font and Paragraph groups on the Home tab.

Tip 7: Insert images into your documents

Graphics are a great way to break up blocks of text, making your documents more visually appealing and easier to read. You can use images to create fliers, brochures, greetings cards and more. Check out the templates that are available from the File>New menu to get more ideas.

1 Click Insert.

2 Click your document to place an insertion point.

3 Click Clip Art in the Illustrations group.

4 Type a keyword in the Search for box to search for a specific image.

5 Click one of the resulting images to add it to your document.

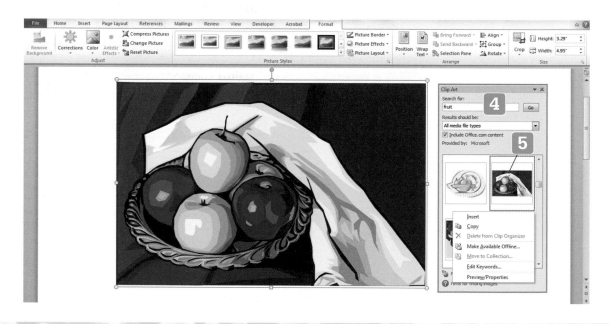

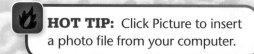
HOT TIP: Click Picture to insert a photo file from your computer.

? **DID YOU KNOW?**

You can find thousands of free clip art files online both at Office.com and other websites. Just make sure that you read the rights and usage policies if you are going to use them in public documents.

Tip 8: Use the spelling and grammar checker to eliminate typos

Nothing says 'unprofessional' like spelling errors and typos in a report or résumé. You can use Word's Spelling and Grammar checker to review your text for wrong spellings, incorrect punctuation and improper capitalisation, amongst other common mistakes.

1 Click Review.

2 Click Spelling and Grammar from the Proofing group.

3 Select an appropriate replacement from Word's suggestions or click Ignore Once to go to the next word.

4 Click Close to exit.

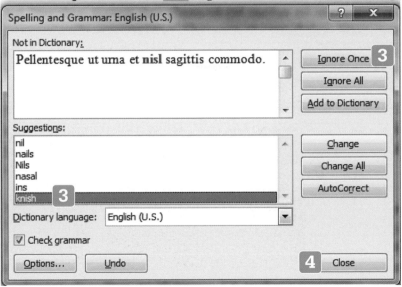

DID YOU KNOW?
Clicking Add to Dictionary adds your word to your custom dictionary. You can add and remove words from the custom dictionary by clicking Custom Dictionaries in the File>Options>Proofing menu.

HOT TIP: Untick the Check Grammar box if you only want Word to check spelling.

Tip 9: Use Track Changes for revisions

Keeping track of document revisions can be tricky, especially if you are receiving input from multiple editors. Track Changes helps you keep edits organised by letting you know what was changed and by whom.

1 Click Review.

2 Click Track Changes in the Tracking group to turn tracking on.

3 Edit your document and your changes will appear in another colour and underlined.

4 Click Track Changes again to turn tracking off.

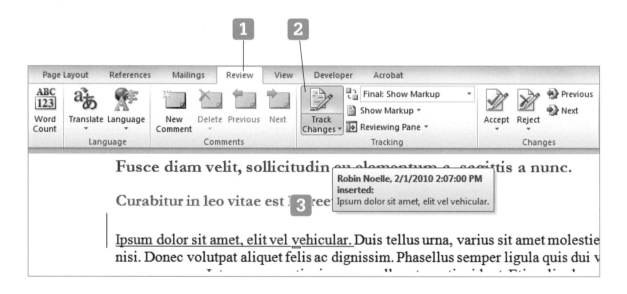

HOT TIP: You can change the way your name appears as an author in tracked changes by clicking on the Track Changes arrow and selecting Change User Name; alternatively change it in the Personalize your Copy of Office section in Word's options (File>Options>General).

Tip 10: Use Word to convert documents to PDF

PDF is the most popular document format for downloadable files. One reason is because anyone can read PDF documents by downloading a free copy of Adobe Reader.

1 Click File.

2 Click Print.

3 Select Adobe PDF from the drop-down printer menu.

4 Click Print to 'print' your document to a PDF file.

5 Select a Save location from the resulting menu.

6 Click Save.

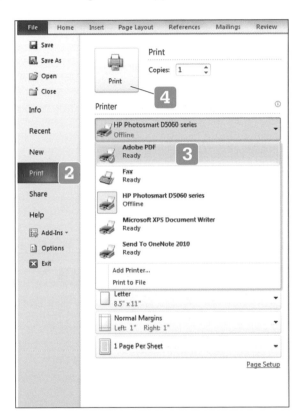

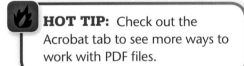
HOT TIP: Check out the Acrobat tab to see more ways to work with PDF files.

WHAT DOES THIS MEAN?

PDF: This stands for Portable Document Format and was developed by Adobe Systems. It was developed so that people could create and view documents regardless of their operating system and computer platform.

1 Getting to know Word

Introduction

Chances are that if you've ever done any word processing on a computer, you've used some version of Microsoft Word. It's part of the most popular productivity suite in the world, Microsoft Office. While each new version may look a little different and have new or enhanced features, the basics of Word remain the same.

You'll access the main features of Word 2010 from the 'Ribbon', a term coined by Microsoft for the tools that run across the top of your screen. In this chapter you'll explore the Ribbon, learn how to view and navigate documents, and learn how to get help both online and through the Office 2010 Help menu.

Installing and activating Microsoft Office

You can install Microsoft Office from a disk or via a download from the Internet. Make sure that you've located the product key before you start your installation.

1 Insert the Microsoft Office installation disk into your CD/DVD drive. Wait while the auto-run feature of the disk starts.

2 Enter your product key found either with your computer documentation or on the packaging with your Office 2010 disk. Then press Continue.

3 Select whether you want to upgrade from a previously installed version of Office or if you want to customise your installation.

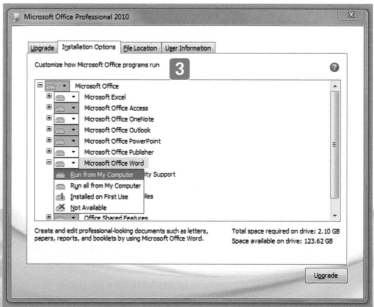

HOT TIP: Choose upgrade to delete all previous versions of Office programs. Choose Customise to keep previous versions or to manually select which applications you want to install (and those that you don't).

4 Finish the installation and reboot your system when prompted.

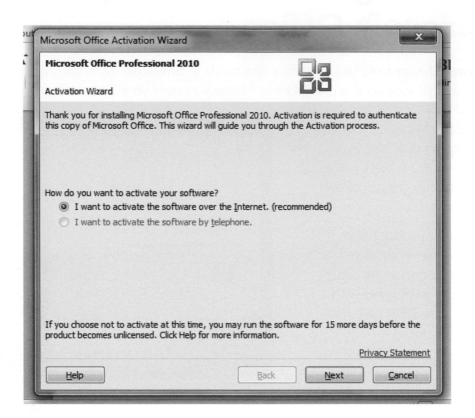

Opening Word

Once Word is installed, you will find it in the Programs menu of your computer. You can easily access it from the Start button or create a shortcut to it on the desktop. There are several ways to open Word.

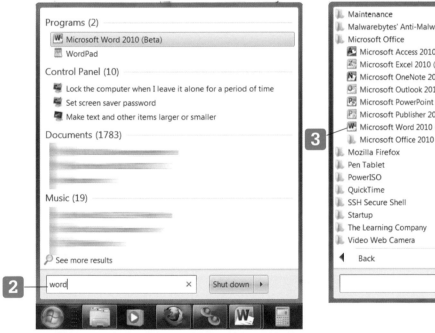

1 Double-click the Word icon on your desktop.

2 Open the Start menu and type 'Word' into the search bar. Select the Word 2010 program from the results.

3 Open the Start menu and select All Programs>Microsoft Office>Word 2010.

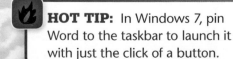

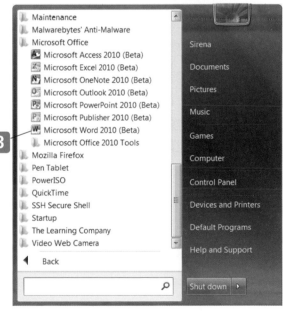

HOT TIP: In Windows 7, pin Word to the taskbar to launch it with just the click of a button.

HOT TIP: Type Word in the search bar of your Start menu to find Word quickly without having to use the All Programs menu in Windows.

Exploring the Ribbon

The Ribbon is the bar that runs along the top of your screen when Word is open. You will notice that it is a series of tabs that you can click to access the functions within. The various tools available in each tab are arranged into groups. This is where you will call up the majority of Word's features.

1 Locate the Home tab. This contains the basic formatting options for your Word documents, such as font, text effects like underline, and bold and spacing options.

2 Locate the Insert tab. The Insert tab allows you to add graphics, headers and footers, or insert special symbols.

3 Locate the Page Layout tab. The Page Layout contains options for setting your margins, changing indents and spacing, and aligning text around graphics.

4 Locate the References tab. The References tab is where you add a table of contents, insert citations or create a bibliography.

5 The Mailings tab will help you set up a mailing list and create labels and envelopes.

6 The Review tab is very important. Here you can check your spelling, track changes and translate documents into other languages.

7 The View tab is helpful when you want to change between writing and viewing how your document will look when printed or displayed on the Web.

8 The Acrobat tab will help you turn your Word document into a PDF file.

HOT TIP: You can quickly move between the Ribbon tabs with just a few keystrokes. Press F10 or Alt to activate the Ribbon and then use the arrow keys on your keyboard to tab through them.

Minimising and restoring the Ribbon

The Ribbon is designed to give you quick access to the most popular Word features. Normally it's open and the options under each tab are visible. To reduce screen clutter, you can minimise the Ribbon so that only the tabs appear.

1 Use Control-F1 to hide and restore the Ribbon.

2 Select the small arrow in the upper right corner of Word.

3 Selecting it again will restore the Ribbon.

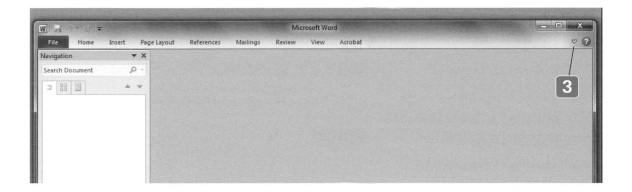

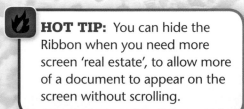

HOT TIP: You can hide the Ribbon when you need more screen 'real estate', to allow more of a document to appear on the screen without scrolling.

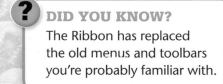

DID YOU KNOW?
The Ribbon has replaced the old menus and toolbars you're probably familiar with.

Using the File menu

The File menu is a critical area to explore. Here you can open, close and save documents as well as create new documents. You can also access the Word Help system, view information about open documents and set permissions for who can view and edit your files.

1 Select the File tab from the Ribbon. You'll see the standard file menu options, including Save, Save As, Open, Close, New, Print, Help and Exit. Other information available from this tab includes:

- Info: This panel shows you, under compatibility mode, whether your document is compatible with the most recent version of Office, Permissions information on who can change or copy your document and what other versions of this document are available, if any. You can also change the permissions settings and check for issues related to sharing documents, as shown here.

- Recent: This shows you a list of your most recently opened documents.

- Share: Provides you with options for sharing your document with others.

- Add-Ins: Manage your add-ins here.

- Options: You can change the options for Microsoft Word here.

2 Click the other tabs once to see what changes appear in the interface. You'll explore those tabs later.

 HOT TIP: You can access the File menu quickly by pressing Alt-F on your keyboard.

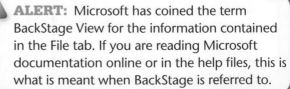 **ALERT:** Microsoft has coined the term BackStage View for the information contained in the File tab. If you are reading Microsoft documentation online or in the help files, this is what is meant when BackStage is referred to.

Navigating Word with shortcuts

Shortcuts are keystrokes that allow you to perform tasks and access features in Word without using your touchpad or mouse.

You should memorise the most common shortcuts in Word as you will be using them often: they are great time savers. They are:

- Ctrl + X = Cut selected text
- Ctrl + C = Copy selected text
- Ctrl + V = Paste text from clipboard
- Ctrl + S = Save document
- Ctrl + P = Print document
- Ctrl + F = Find

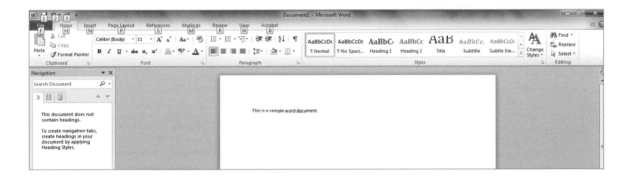

 DID YOU KNOW?

Most shortcuts use the Control (Ctrl) key or the Alt key in conjunction with other keys on the keyboard. For example, if you see a command that says Ctrl-W, that means press and hold the Control key down and then press the W key to execute the command.

HOT TIP: Microsoft Word includes a feature called 'Key Tips'. When you press the Alt key, keyboard shortcuts will be highlighted on your screen. Select the appropriate letter to access that shortcut. For example, press Alt while in the main Word workspace. Then press F to get to the File menu and N to create a new document. You can turn off the Key Tips by pressing Alt a second time.

Navigating a document in Word

If you are working on a single page document, it's pretty easy to navigate through it using your mouse or the arrow keys, but what if you have dozens or hundreds of pages to go through? In Word, there are several ways to navigate through lengthy documents.

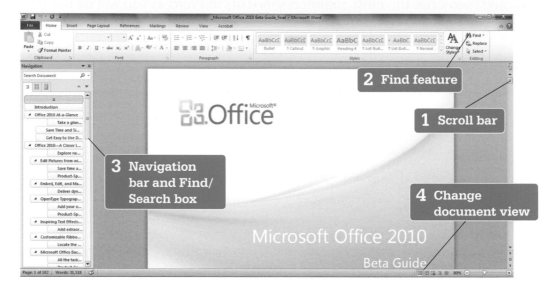

1. Use Page Up and Page Down on your keyboard to quickly turn pages in your document or use the mouse or touchpad to move the scroll bar.

2. Use the Find feature (Ctrl-F) to quickly locate and navigate to words or phrases in your document.

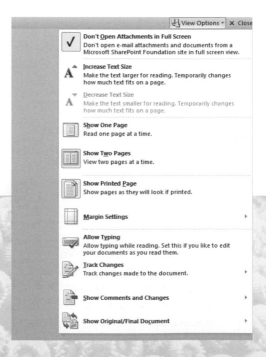

3. Use the navigation pane to browse headings or pages.

4. Change your view to Full Screen Reading to quickly page through a document using arrows.

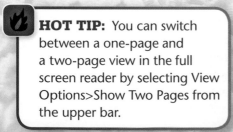

HOT TIP: You can switch between a one-page and a two-page view in the full screen reader by selecting View Options>Show Two Pages from the upper bar.

Zooming in and out of a document

Sometimes you will need to zoom in and out of your document, to read very small text, for example. You can do this in one of three ways:

1 Use the zoom scroll bar located in the bottom right corner of your screen. Use the – to zoom out and + to zoom in.

2 Go to the View tab and select Zoom to open the Zoom dialogue box.

3 Use the wheel feature on your mouse, if it has one. Roll the wheel upwards to zoom out and down to zoom in.

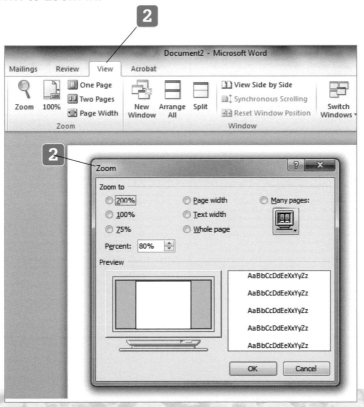

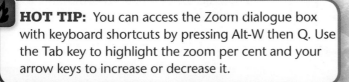

HOT TIP: You can access the Zoom dialogue box with keyboard shortcuts by pressing Alt-W then Q. Use the Tab key to highlight the zoom per cent and your arrow keys to increase or decrease it.

Using the full screen reading view

When you need to read a document, often it is easier when done in the full screen view. This removes a lot of the screen clutter and allows you to view and navigate through a document more easily. There are two distinct ways:

1 Enter full screen reading view by selecting it in the status bar at the bottom of your screen or by selecting View>Full Screen Reading from the Ribbon.

2 Turn pages by using the arrows at the top of the screen or the ones in the corners of the pages.

HOT TIP: To quickly move to another page in the Full Screen View, press the page number on your keyboard and hit ENTER.

DID YOU KNOW?

You have access to functions commonly used in the full screen reading view at the top of the page. These include highlighting text, adding a comment, printing and saving.

Using the print view

Occasionally it's useful to be able to view how your document will look when it's finally printed. You can do this by accessing the print view.

1 Locate the print view icon on the status bar at the bottom of your screen.

2 Go to View>Print Layout from the Ribbon.

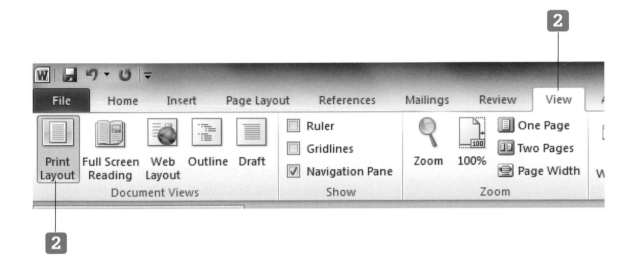

? **DID YOU KNOW?**

Print view is the view most often used for creating documents. Use the zoom feature to fit the document to your screen to see how your printed page will look.

Using the Web view

If you want to see what your text will look like in a Web browser, you can use the Web layout view to check it out.

1 Access the Web layout icon from the status bar at the bottom of your screen.

2 Go to View>Web Layout from the Ribbon tabs.

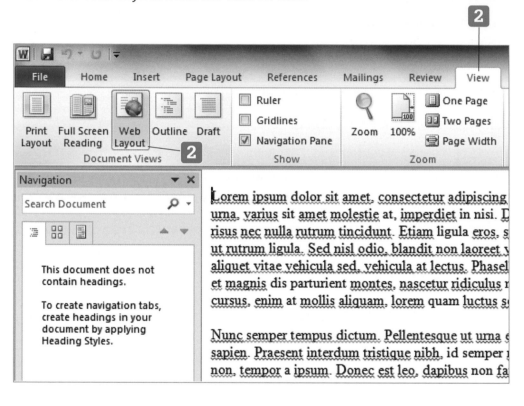

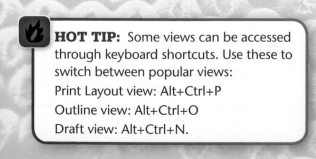
HOT TIP: Some views can be accessed through keyboard shortcuts. Use these to switch between popular views:

Print Layout view: Alt+Ctrl+P

Outline view: Alt+Ctrl+O

Draft view: Alt+Ctrl+N.

Locating the Quick Access menu

The Quick Access menu is located at the top of your screen and gives you quick and easy access to the most commonly used functions, such as Save and Undo. You can easily customise this menu to include the items that you use most frequently.

1 Look for the Quick Access menu in the upper left corner of your screen.

2 Pull down on the small arrow to access the menu options.

3 Click each item that you wish to appear in the Quick Access menu. A tickmark will appear by the ones that you have selected. Now you will see your selected items at the top of the screen, ready for you to use.

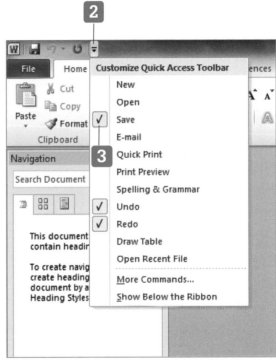

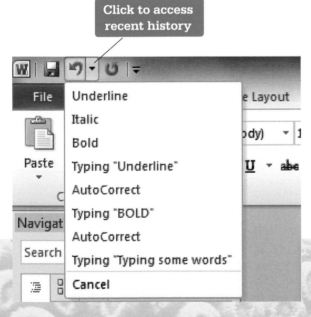

Click to access recent history

HOT TIP: Do you see the small arrow next to the Undo icon on the Quick Access menu? Click the arrow to access your recent history. From here, you can select just how far back you want to undo!

Finding and using the Help menu

Microsoft Office provides extensive help files for every feature and function provided by the suite. Word is no different. You can easily access the Help menu to find answers to almost any question that you have.

1 Click the small question mark in the upper right corner of your screen. This brings up the Help menu.

2 Access Help from the File Menu on the Ribbon.

? DID YOU KNOW?
To use the Help menu, type what you are looking for into the search bar at the top of the dialogue box or select a topic from the popular topics that are provided.

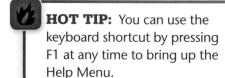

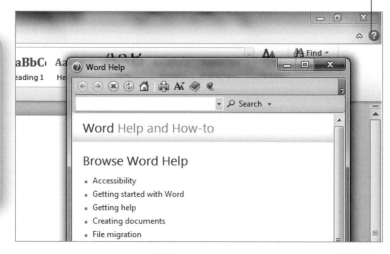

🔥 HOT TIP: You can use the keyboard shortcut by pressing F1 at any time to bring up the Help Menu.

? DID YOU KNOW?
To access help on specific functions, hover your mouse cursor over the button that you need help with. A dialogue box will appear telling you the name of the function and suggesting that you press F1 for additional help.

Using Microsoft Office help online

If your computer is connected to the Internet, using the Help menu will automatically give you access to the online help files. You can also find a wealth of information on the Microsoft Office homepage. Visit http://office.microsoft.com/ to find more help and how-to information, download clipart and templates or interact with other Office users in the Office Community Forums.

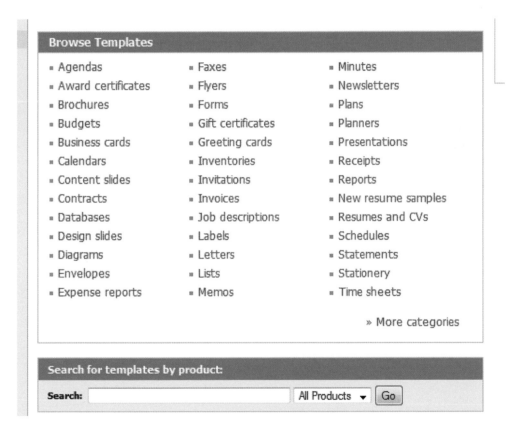

Browse Templates

- Agendas
- Award certificates
- Brochures
- Budgets
- Business cards
- Calendars
- Content slides
- Contracts
- Databases
- Design slides
- Diagrams
- Envelopes
- Expense reports

- Faxes
- Flyers
- Forms
- Gift certificates
- Greeting cards
- Inventories
- Invitations
- Invoices
- Job descriptions
- Labels
- Letters
- Lists
- Memos

- Minutes
- Newsletters
- Plans
- Planners
- Presentations
- Receipts
- Reports
- New resume samples
- Resumes and CVs
- Schedules
- Statements
- Stationery
- Time sheets

» More categories

Search for templates by product:

Search: [   ] All Products ▼ [Go]

? DID YOU KNOW?

There are hundreds of templates online for everything from greeting cards to gift certificates. All are free for you to download and use.

 HOT TIP: Check out the Office community forums if you can't find answers in the Help menu. The chances are that someone else has posed the same question before. You may find your answers there!

2 Customising with Word options

Introduction

Microsoft Word offers myriad opportunities to customise and personalise your word processing experience. There are a variety of options that you can utilise to make your user experience best suited to your work style.

You can select Word Options from the File menu on the Ribbon. From these options settings, you can optimise your Quick Access menu, change the language of Word and alter your printing settings. It's worth taking the time to fully explore what options are available. What you find might surprise you!

Enable the Mini Toolbar

The Mini Toolbar is a convenient way to quickly access formatting options in your document. When this feature is enabled, a small toolbar will appear just above any highlighted text, allowing you to change several of the most common font and paragraph formatting options.

1 Click the File menu.

2 Click Options.

3 Tick the Mini Toolbar box to turn this option on and untick it to turn it off.

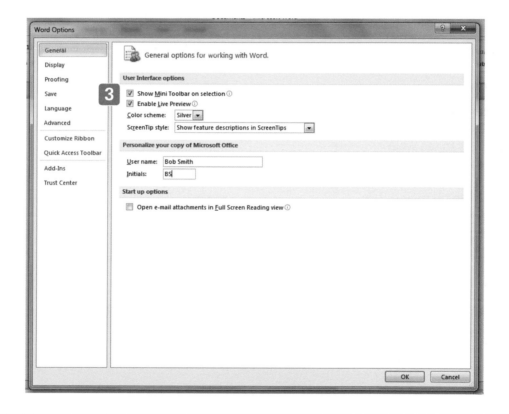

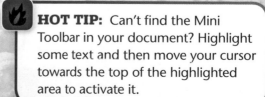

HOT TIP: The formatting options on the Mini Toolbar are the same as those that appear on the Ribbon. Some people find them handy. If you don't, just turn off the toolbar and they're gone for good!

HOT TIP: Can't find the Mini Toolbar in your document? Highlight some text and then move your cursor towards the top of the highlighted area to activate it.

Use Live Preview

The Live Preview button lets you see what potential changes to your document will look like prior to applying them. For example, if you select text in your document and then hover your cursor over a different text style or font, you can see what those changes will look like.

1 Type some text into a new document.

2 Position the mouse over any of the Styles on the Home tab.

3 Continue to reposition the mouse to preview other styles.

4 Click any style to apply it.

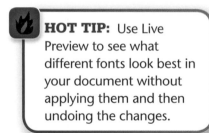

HOT TIP: Use Live Preview to see what different fonts look best in your document without applying them and then undoing the changes.

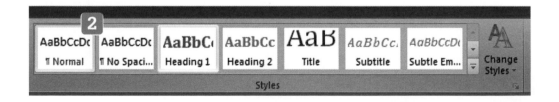

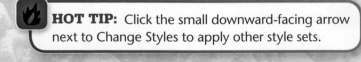

HOT TIP: Click the small downward-facing arrow next to Change Styles to apply other style sets.

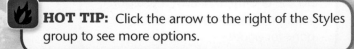

HOT TIP: Click the arrow to the right of the Styles group to see more options.

Stop showing Screen Tips (or show them)

Screen Tips appear when you hover your cursor over the various buttons in Word. For example, if you hover over the icon for bulleted lists, Word will tell you what the button is called and how to use it. You can opt to leave Screen Tips on, to only see the button name or to turn them off altogether.

1 Click the File Menu tab.

2 Click Options.

3 Change the default setting for showing Screen Tips using the drop-down menu.

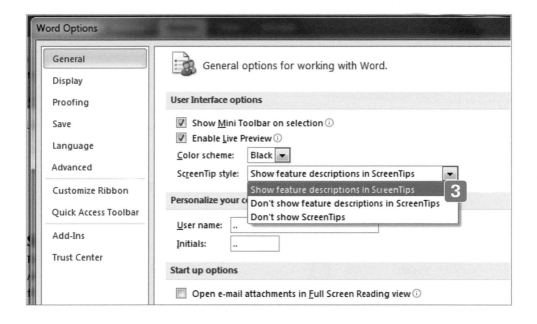

 HOT TIP: Use Screen Tips to find out more about buttons and icons that you've never used. You just might find something useful during your exploration!

 DID YOU KNOW?
Screen Tips show you the button name and its function while Key Tips help you access the features of Word using only your keyboard.

Customise your copy of Microsoft Office

You can personalise your copy of Office in many other ways. For instance, you can insert the default author name that will appear in the document information for all items created with your copy of Word.

1 Click the File Menu tab.

2 Click Options.

3 Type your name where it says User name.

4 Type your initials in the Initials box.

HOT TIP: You can change the author name or add additional authors to a document during the Save process.

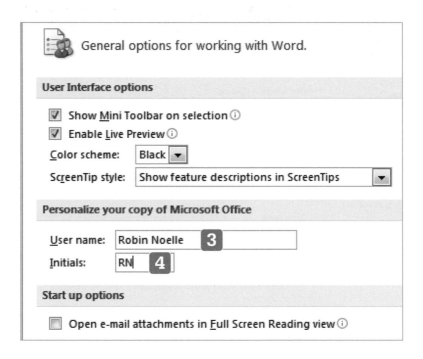

General options for working with Word.

User Interface options

☑ Show Mini Toolbar on selection ⓘ
☑ Enable Live Preview ⓘ
Color scheme: Black ▾
ScreenTip style: Show feature descriptions in ScreenTips ▾

Personalize your copy of Microsoft Office

User name: Robin Noelle **3**
Initials: RN **4**

Start up options

☐ Open e-mail attachments in Full Screen Reading view ⓘ

ALERT: If you open a document or template that was created by someone else, chances are that their name is in the author box. Be sure to change this to your name if you customise or otherwise change the document.

Customise and move the Quick Access toolbar

The Quick Access toolbar gives you easy access to functions that you use all the time, like Open, Save and Undo. You can customise this toolbar to include the items that you use the most and remove the ones that you don't.

1. Click the arrow on the Quick Access toolbar.

2. Select the items that you wish to appear in your Quick Access Menu.

> **HOT TIP:** The Quick Access toolbar is in the upper left corner of your screen.

3. Click Show Below the Ribbon if you want the Quick Access bar to be located below the main Word Ribbon instead of the default location above it.

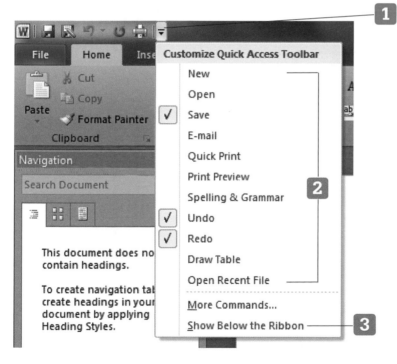

> **HOT TIP:** A tickmark in a small box will appear by the ones you have selected. Click the box again to deselect an item.

> **? DID YOU KNOW?**
> You can also access the Quick Access customisation screen by selecting File>Options>Quick Access Toolbar.

> **HOT TIP:** Add all of your favourite Word commands to the Quick Access Menu and then minimise the Ribbon to create an uncluttered workspace without losing access to the functions you use most.

Customise the Ribbon and keyboard shortcuts

The Ribbon is designed to give you quick access to the most popular Word features. Normally the Ribbon is open and the options under each tab are visible. You can add or delete commands for these tabs and the groups they contain, or assign new keyboard shortcuts to your favourite commands by using the Customise Ribbon dialogue box.

1 Click the File Menu.

2 Click Options and then Customise Ribbon.

3 Select the commands you wish to add from the first column and then use the second column to navigate to where you want to add the command. Use the + and – to expand and reduce the menus.

DID YOU KNOW?

To save your keyboard shortcuts for a specific document, change the setting in the Customize Keyboard dialogue box from Normal to your current document.

4 Click Add to add a command to a section. You can use the Remove button to remove a command that you've added.

5 Click the Customise button at the bottom of the dialogue box. Assign keyboard shortcuts to commands or change existing shortcuts.

6 Use the Import/Export button to export your settings for use with other computers.

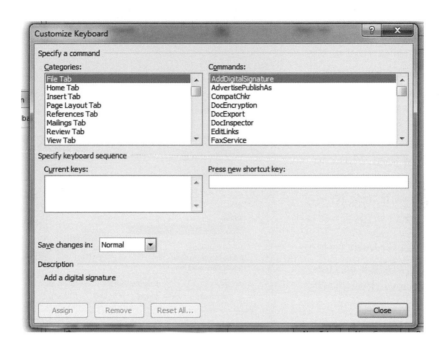

 HOT TIP: Export your settings and save them on a jump drive so they can be easily loaded onto your computer at work or anywhere else where you use Word.

Setting the default font

The default font for Microsoft Word is Calibri but many companies prefer to use another standard font like Times New Roman or Chicago. You can change the default font to anything you like and it will be used in all newly created documents.

1 Locate the Font box in the Home tab on the Ribbon.

2 Click the small arrow in the lower right corner, under the font colour drop-down menu.

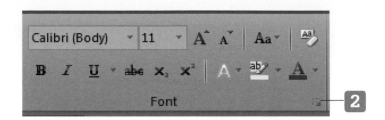

3 Make your selections for your desired font. You can change the style, colour and size of your font to anything you choose.

4 Select Set As Default to lock in your font choice as the default for new documents.

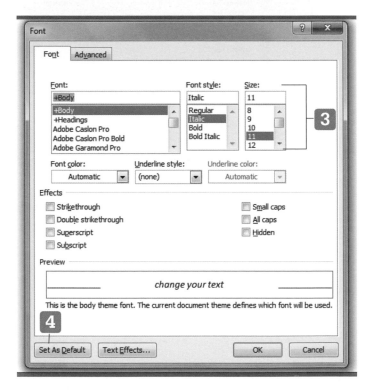

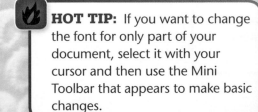

HOT TIP: If you want to change the font for only part of your document, select it with your cursor and then use the Mini Toolbar that appears to make basic changes.

? DID YOU KNOW?

A serif font has small finishing marks at the ends of the letters while a sans serif font does not. It's generally believed that sans serif fonts read better online while serif fonts are better for printed materials.

Change the language of Word

At some point you may wish to use Microsoft Word in another language, for example, if you live in a bilingual household or if you work for an international company and handle documents in a foreign language. You can purchase and install a variety of language packs for Word that will allow you not only to write but to check spelling and grammar in almost any language.

1 From the File Menu, click Options>Language.

2 Under Choose Editing Languages, review the languages you currently have installed and enabled.

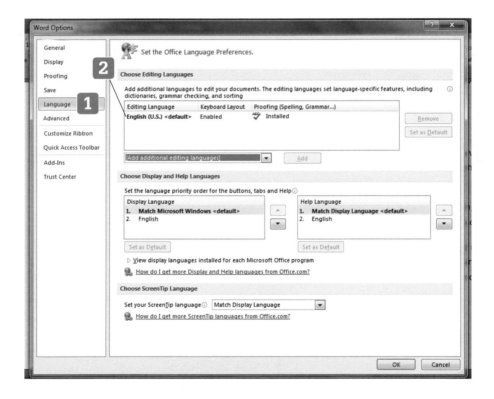

 HOT TIP: As you select the language you want, it will appear in the box above. This will show you if it is installed.

3 Select other languages for editing tasks like spelling and grammar from the drop-down menu.

4 Select your display language from the second portion of the dialogue box. By default, it's set to whatever language Windows was installed in.

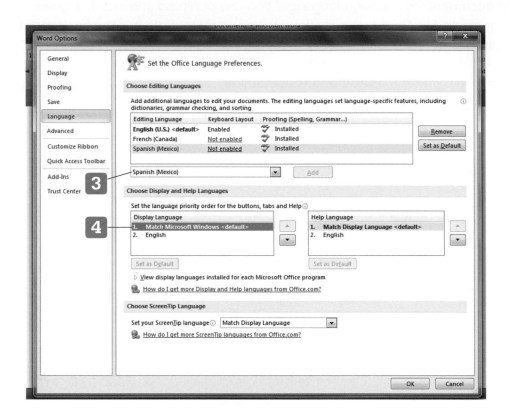

 HOT TIP: You can't use a language if it isn't enabled. Enable the language by clicking on the Enable link and you will be able to set it as a default or use it in specific documents.

 **DID YOU KNOW?**

Some language packs include multiple languages. For example, the Spanish language pack includes proofing tools not only for Spanish but for Basque, Catalan, English, French, Galician and Portuguese.

Create and use a custom dictionary

While Microsoft Office has an extensive dictionary, it doesn't include every word in every language nor does it contain jargon, technical terms, slang or proper names. You can easily create your own custom dictionaries to include these words and prevent Spell Check from flagging them erroneously.

1 Click the File menu.

2 Click Options and then click Proofing.

3 Click the Custom Dictionaries button.

4 Add and remove custom dictionaries including foreign language dictionaries.

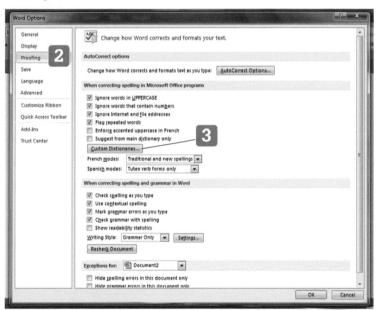

HOT TIP: Did you add a misspelled word to your custom dictionary? You can edit your added word list from the Custom Dictionary dialogue box.

Change your AutoCorrect settings

AutoCorrect can save you a lot of time if you use it correctly. You can set it up so Word automatically corrects words that you consistently misspelled or to add capitalisation to a proper noun like a day of the week. Check the appropriate boxes to select the options that you want to employ, including:

- correcting two capitalised letters in a row.

- automatically fixing transposed letters.

- automatically capitalising specified proper nouns.

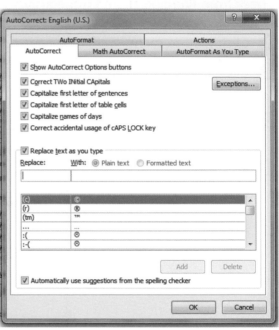

 DID YOU KNOW?

You can also use the AutoCorrect feature to change words into mathematical symbols.

 HOT TIP: You can use AutoCorrect to change a word into a symbol, like changing TM into the trademark symbol ™.

 ALERT: Be careful when adding words to AutoCorrect. It might seem like a good idea to use AutoCorrect to add the special characters in the word résumé until you want to use the word resume.

Creating a document exception in Spell Check

Sometimes if you are creating a document with lots of acronyms or other specialised terms, you may want to skip the spelling and grammar check altogether. You can create an exception for a single document and eliminate those little red lines that appear under what Word thinks are misspellings.

1. Click the File Menu.

2. Click Options.

3. Click Proofing.

4. Scroll to the bottom of the box and select which document you want to make an exception for.

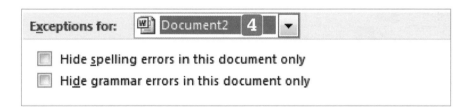

 HOT TIP: You can choose whether to ignore spelling errors, grammar errors or both.

 HOT TIP: If you don't want to turn off Spell Check completely for a document, you can untick the Check Spelling as You Type option and then run the spell checker manually when you have finished typing.

Customise how documents are saved

If you've been using computers for a while, you've probably heard the old adage, 'save early, save often'. Few things are more frustrating than losing a document you've spent hours of time on due to a computer crash. Fortunately, you can customise your save options to auto-save and recover any documents you are working on.

1 Click the File button.

2 Click Options, and click Save.

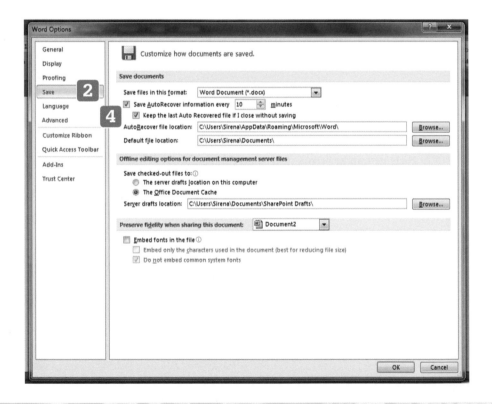

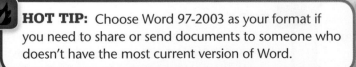

HOT TIP: Choose Word 97-2003 as your format if you need to share or send documents to someone who doesn't have the most current version of Word.

3 From the drop-down menu, select a Save As format.

4 Set the frequency of your auto-recover by selecting the appropriate time intervals. You can also select where these copies are stored by selecting another file path.

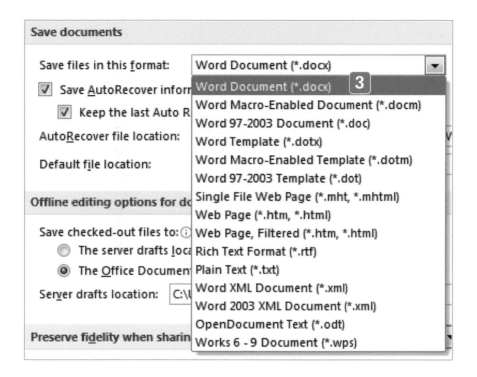

 HOT TIP: Use the keyboard shortcut Ctrl-S to save your document quickly.

 DID YOU KNOW?

From the Save Options you can change the default location where your documents are saved. The default is to My Documents but you can set it to any location on your computer.

Change your print settings

By default, Word is set to print a clean document, showing only the printed text and any embedded graphics. You can change these settings to include drawings made in Word as well as background images and colours.

1 Click the File button and click Options.

2 Click Display.

3 Under Printing options, select the options you wish to enable. Click the tickbox again to deselect an item.

4 Click OK to verify your changes.

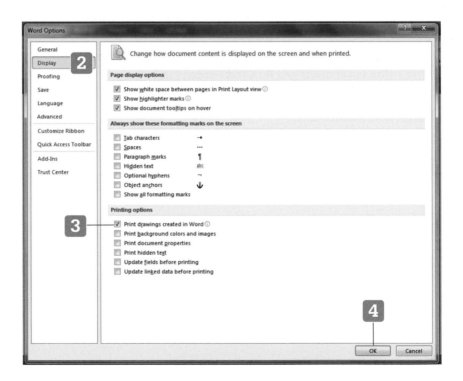

 **DID YOU KNOW?**

You can download even more templates from the Office.com website, all for free!

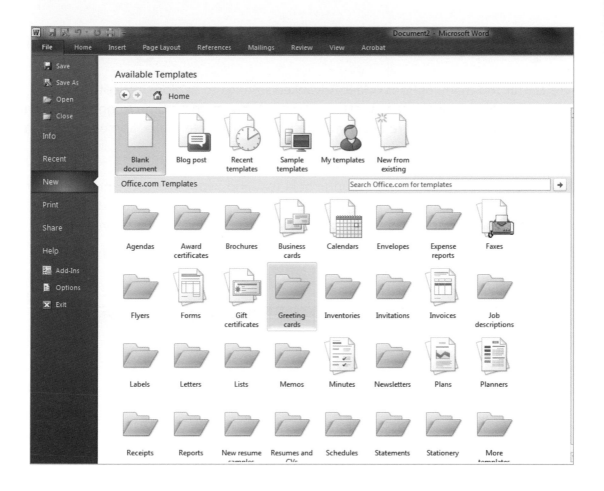

HOT TIP: You can find stationery and other templates that use background colour by selecting New from the File Menu and browsing the Office.com templates that appear.

Explore Advanced settings

There are far too many options under Advanced settings to explore in-depth in this chapter, or even over several chapters, so it's worth taking some time to go through the settings yourself to see if there are any alterations you'd like to make. Some of the more helpful settings to explore include:

1 Editing options: here you can change how text and hyperlinks are handled in your document. You can decide if you want to insert or replace selected text by typing, whether you can drag and drop text and what the default style is for your text.

2 Cut, copy, and paste: change the default settings for how text is handled during cutting, copying and pasting.

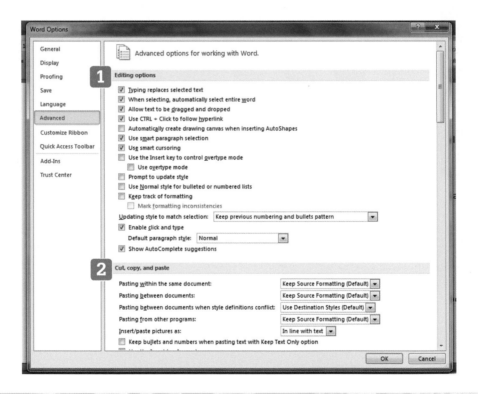

HOT TIP: Explore the Smart Cut and Paste settings to allow Word to automatically format your pasted text. For example, with Smart Cut and Paste, a table pasted into a different Word document can either retain its original formatting or Word can automatically adjust it to match the formatting of the destination document.

3 Image Size and Quality: set the default resolution of embedded graphics here.

4 Display: Set how many recent documents appear in the Recent tab of the File menu, set your standard unit of measurement and determine whether keyboard shortcuts appear in the Screen Tips.

5 Show document content: you can opt to show text animation, crop marks and other content in your document.

3 Creating basic Word documents

Introduction

Microsoft Word 2010 won't be of much use to you if you don't know how to create documents. More than just a text editor, Word 2010 can be used to create a variety of documents from the plainest personal letter to complex reports filled with graphics, charts and rotating 3D text effects. This chapter will explore how to create a basic Word document and apply simple formatting. You'll also learn how to manipulate those documents in terms of opening, closing and saving.

Creating a new blank document

While there are many templates to choose from in Word 2010, most of the time, you'll probably want to start with a new, blank document.

1 Click File.

2 Click New.

🔥 **HOT TIP:** Use the keyboard shortcut, Ctrl-N to quickly open a new blank document.

? DID YOU KNOW?

You can create many types of blank documents in Word, including blank blog posts and webpages.

Creating a document from a template

You can use templates to easily add a professional looking design to your document. Templates include graphics, colour schemes and text boxes. All you need to do is add your text in the spaces provided.

1 Click File.

2 Click New.

3 Click Sample Templates.

4 Choose a template and double-click to open it.

HOT TIP: The Microsoft Word website contains hundreds of templates that you can download and use for free.

DID YOU KNOW?
Microsoft isn't the only place you can find templates for Word. Type 'word templates' into your favourite search engine and see what comes up!

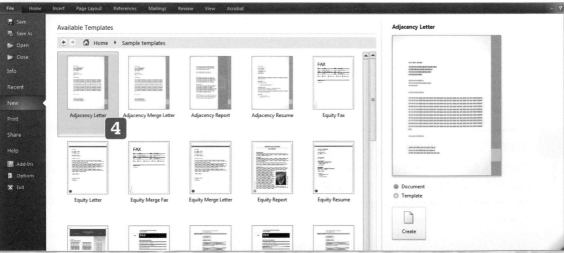

Creating a new document from an existing one

You can save a lot of time designing your document if you have a copy of one that is similar to the one you want to create. This is a great feature to use if you regularly create the same type of document and want to keep the formatting and/or graphics the same.

1 Click the File.

2 Click New.

3 Click New from existing.

4 Browse for the document you want to use.

5 Click Open.

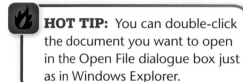

HOT TIP: You can double-click the document you want to open in the Open File dialogue box just as in Windows Explorer.

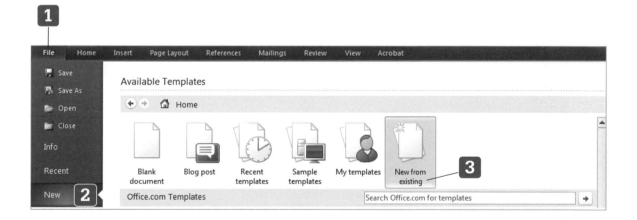

DID YOU KNOW?

You can also use Key Tips to open a new document from an existing one. Just press ALT-F to display the Tips and press N to go to New Documents.

Opening an existing document

You can use these steps to open an existing document that is on your computer or a portable flash drive.

1 Click File.

2 Click Open.

3 Browse for the document you want to open.

4 Click the document icon.

5 Click Open.

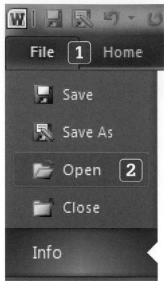

HOT TIP: You can also use the keyboard shortcut Ctrl-O to open a document.

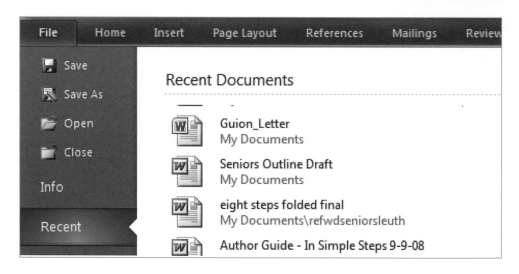

DID YOU KNOW?

If you've opened a document recently it should appear in the Recent tab in the File menu.

Saving documents

After all your hard work on your new Word document, you'll want to save it to your hard disk so you can access it again.

1 Click File.

2 Click Save.

3 Name your document and select a Save location from the open dialogue box.

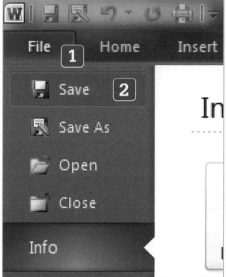

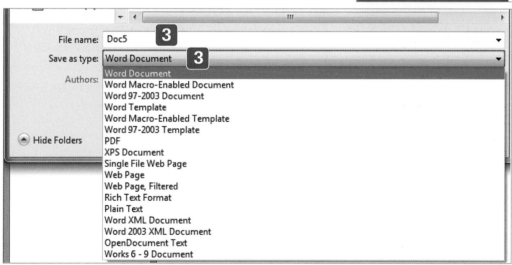

HOT TIP: You can also quickly save your document from the Quick Access menu at the top of your screen or by pressing Ctrl-S on your keyboard.

? **DID YOU KNOW?**

You can save Word documents in many formats including plain or rich text and as an HTML file.

Saving a copy of an open document

Sometimes you want to save a copy of a document without altering the original. You can do this using the Save As feature. It allows you to save a copy of a document as a separate file and, if you want, as a different file type than the original.

1 Click File.

2 Click Save As.

3 Browse to the location where you want to save your document.

4 Type a new name in the text box.

5 Select the format you want to save your document in from the drop-down menu.

6 Click Save.

? DID YOU KNOW?

Choose Word 97-2003 as your file format if you need to send your document to someone with a previous version of Word.

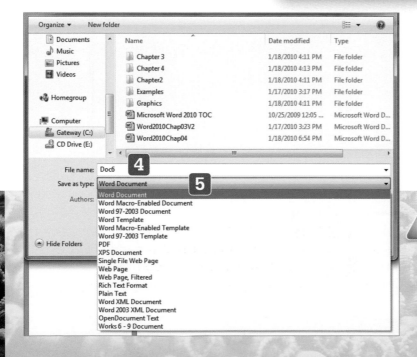

! ALERT: Don't forget to check that the author name is correct when you Save As, if someone else created the original document.

Selecting text with the mouse

Now that you have mastered the basics, it's time to start working in your new document. Before you can make changes to your work, you need to learn how to select the text that you want to change. The most common way to do this is with the mouse.

Placing your mouse on the document screen turns it into a precision cursor for inputting text.

1 Place your cursor at the beginning or end of the text you want to select.

2 Drag your mouse over the text while holding down the mouse button to select the text.

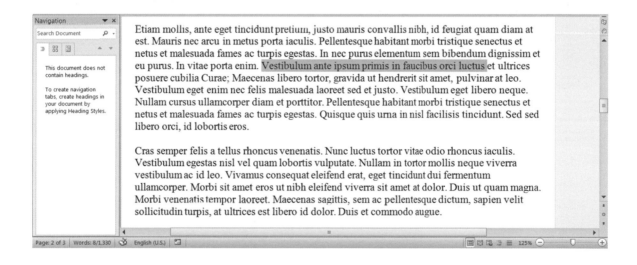

 HOT TIP: To select a single word, just place your cursor over the word and double-click!

 HOT TIP: To select a whole sentence, place your cursor over the sentence and press the Ctrl key when you click your mouse button.

Selecting text blocks with the mouse

You can select text blocks with just a few clicks.

1 Click at the beginning of your text block to place your cursor.

2 Press and hold the shift key.

3 Move your cursor to the end of the text block.

4 Click to select all of the text between the two points.

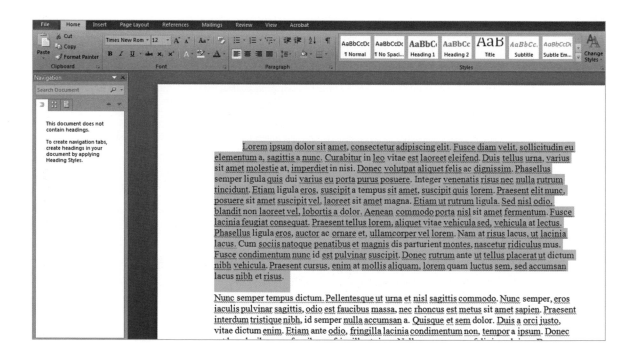

 DID YOU KNOW?

You can move text within your document by selecting it and dragging it where you want to place it.

 HOT TIP: Use Ctrl-X to cut your text and place it on the clipboard so you can paste it in another location within your document or another document altogether.

Selecting text with the keyboard

It can be a hassle for a fast typist to take their hands away from the keyboard to use the mouse, which is why Microsoft has included so many keyboard shortcuts. You can also select text from your keyboard in Word, making selecting a single character or letter much easier than with the mouse.

1 To select one or more characters, use the arrow keys to move your cursor to where you want to place your insertion point. Press Shift and move the arrow keys again to select text to the right or left.

2 To select a whole word, press Ctrl-Shift while moving the arrow keys to select words to the right or left. Keep pressing the arrow keys to select more words.

3 To select to the end of a line, place your insertion point and then press Shift-END on your keyboard.

Lorem ipsum dolor sit amet, consectetur adipiscing elit. Fusce diam velit, sollicitudin eu elementum a, sagittis a nunc. Curabitur in leo vitae est laoreet eleifend. Duis tellus urna, varius sit amet molestie at, imperdiet in nisi. Donec volutpat aliquet felis ac dignissim. Phasellus semper ligula quis dui varius eu porta purus posuere. Integer venenatis risus nec nulla rutrum tincidunt. Etiam ligula eros, suscipit a tempus sit amet, suscipit quis lorem. Praesent elit nunc, posuere sit amet suscipit vel, laoreet sit amet magna. Etiam ut rutrum ligula. Sed nisl odio, blandit non laoreet vel, lobortis a dolor. Aenean commodo porta nisl sit amet fermentum. Fusce lacinia feugiat consequat. Praesent tellus lorem, aliquet vitae vehicula sed, vehicula at lectus. Phasellus ligula eros, auctor ac ornare et, ullamcorper vel lorem. Nam at risus lacus, ut lacinia lacus. Cum sociis natoque penatibus et magnis dis parturient montes, nascetur ridiculus mus. Fusce condimentum nunc id est pulvinar suscipit. Donec rutrum ante ut tellus placerat ut dictum nibh vehicula. Praesent cursus, enim at mollis aliquam, lorem quam luctus sem, sed accumsan lacus nibh et risus.

Nunc semper tempus dictum. Pellentesque ut urna et nisl sagittis commodo. Nunc semper, eros iaculis pulvinar sagittis, odio est faucibus massa, nec rhoncus est metus sit amet sapien. Praesent

 HOT TIP: Experiment with this function to highlight other selections of text. For example, pressing Ctrl-Shift-DOWN will select a whole paragraph below your insertion point as shown here.

 HOT TIP: Need to select all of the text within a document? Use the Ctrl-A shortcut to select all text.

Making multiple selections within a document

You can make formatting changes to text located in different areas within your document all at once by using the Multiple Selection function.

1 Click to position your cursor at the beginning of your first selection.

2 Click and drag to highlight the text you want.

3 Press and hold the Ctrl key.

4 Move your cursor to the next selection.

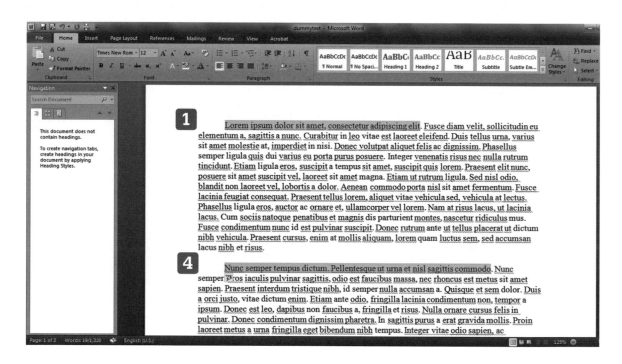

Drag and highlight this text to add it to your highlighted selections.

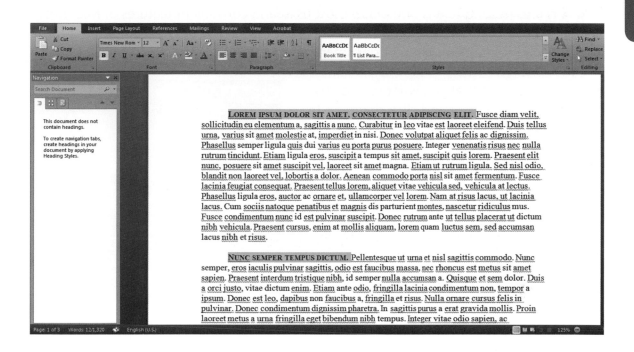

HOT TIP: With your selections highlighted, apply formatting such as bold, italics or small and large capitals. More than one option can be applied. It will only affect your selected text.

ALERT: Keep pressing the Ctrl key until all selections have been made or you will lose your previous selections.

Copying and pasting text

Copying and pasting text is one of the most used and convenient features of Microsoft Word. You can copy and paste text from one part of your document to another or from another source such as a different document or a webpage.

1. Select the text that you want to copy by placing your cursor and click-dragging to highlight it.

2. Click the Home tab on the ribbon.

3. Click Copy.

4. Click within your document to place your cursor where you want to paste the copied text.

5. Click Paste on the Home tab to insert your text.

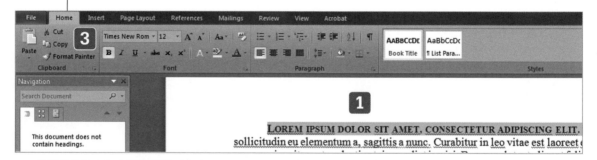

HOT TIP: Use the Ctrl-C keyboard shortcut to quickly copy highlighted text and Ctrl-V to paste it.

DID YOU KNOW?

When you copy or cut text, Word saves it on a virtual clipboard. You can paste it in as many places as you like as long as you don't copy new text to the clipboard.

HOT TIP: Use the Live Preview function to see how your copied text will look in its new place. Use the drop-down menu from the Paste button on the ribbon and hover your cursor over the clipboard icon.

Cutting text

If you don't want to keep the selected text in your document when you paste it somewhere else, you can use the cut function. Cutting removes the text from your document but saves it on the clipboard where it will be available until you cut or copy something else.

1 Select the text that you want to cut by placing your cursor and click-dragging to highlight it.

2 Click Home.

3 Click Cut.

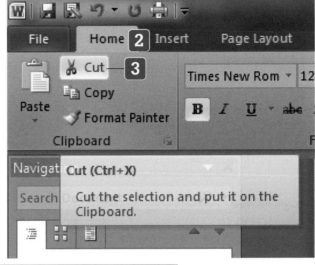

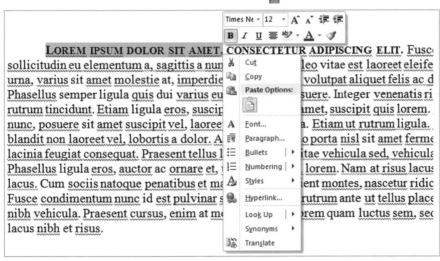

 HOT TIP: Use Ctrl-X to cut text quickly.

? DID YOU KNOW?

You can also access the cut, copy and paste commands via the right-click menu from your mouse. Just highlight your selections and click the right mouse button to see the menu.

Finding specific text within a document

Sometimes you need to find a word or phrase within a long document. You can easily search for anything you're looking for with the Find feature.

1 Click Home.

2 Click Find.

3 Type your search term into the text box on the resulting navigation window.

4 Select the results that you want to view from the Results window.

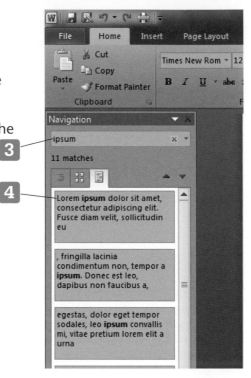

HOT TIP: Use the small arrows near the search box to scroll through your results.

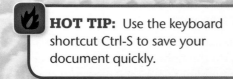

HOT TIP: Use the keyboard shortcut Ctrl-S to save your document quickly.

DID YOU KNOW?

You can select which elements (graphics, comments, etc.) you want to search for from the drop-down menu to the right of the magnifying glass in the search box.

Replacing text

Suppose that you've typed an entire report only to find that you've misspelled a company's name. By using the Replace feature, you can replace all instances of the misspelled word at once.

1 Click Home.

2 Click Replace.

3 Type the word that you want to replace in the Find what box.

4 Type the word that you want to replace it with in the Replace with box.

5 Click Replace to replace a single instance or Replace All to replace all instances.

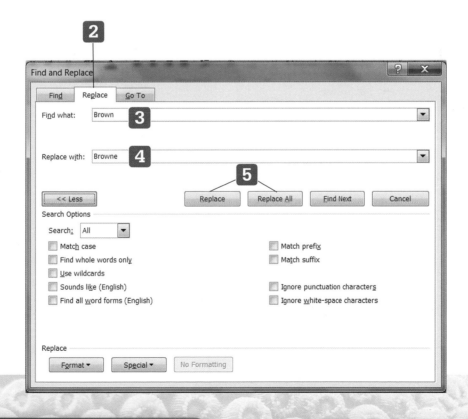

HOT TIP: You don't have to use Replace just for words. You can also use it to insert spaces, symbols or punctuation. For example, you could replace $40 with £40.

DID YOU KNOW?

Click the More button to see even more Find and Replace options.

Changing the font

Word 2010 comes with many fonts to choose from for designing your documents. You can create a document with a single font or mix and match to your heart's content. A few examples are shown here.

1 Click Home.

2 Click the down arrow in the Font name box.

3 Click the font that you want to use.

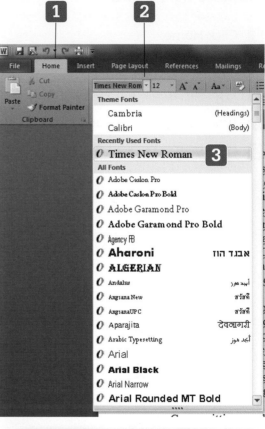

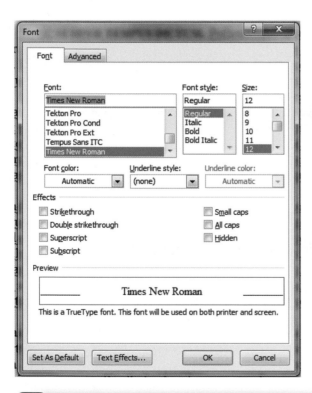

HOT TIP: Use the other buttons in the Font box to add text formatting like italics and bold or to change the size or colour of your text.

HOT TIP: Highlight a text block and then choose a new font from the Font box. This will apply the new font to your selected text.

DID YOU KNOW?

There's a very small arrow in the lower right corner of the Font box on the Home tab. Click this arrow to expand your font options.

DID YOU KNOW?

You can download new and unique fonts online. Type 'free fonts' into your favourite search engine and check out the results!

Using AutoCorrect to replace text

AutoCorrect does exactly what it says it does; it automatically corrects as you type. AutoCorrect is on by default and is handy for correcting typical typos like transposed letters (hte instead of the) or for automatically capitalising the first word in a sentence. You can also use it to automatically replace text, such as replacing an acronym with a full title.

1 Click File.

2 Click Options.

3 Click Proofing> AutoCorrect.

4 Click the Replace text as you type box.

5 Enter the abbreviation you want to use into the Replace text box.

6 Enter what you would like it replaced with in the With text box.

7 Click Add to add it to the queue.

? DID YOU KNOW?

You can use the scroll bar in the AutoCorrect options window to look through the list of AutoCorrect pairs. You can delete any that you do not wish AutoCorrect to use.

🔥 HOT TIP: If AutoCorrect makes a change that you don't like, you can use Ctrl-Z or the Undo button to go back. It won't autocorrect that word again in your open document.

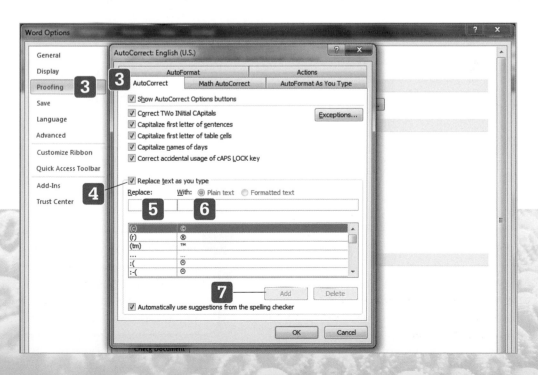

Automatic hyphenation

In the past, when people used typewriters, you had to do a manual return at the end of every page line, but with a word-processing program, it automatically moves down to the next line on the page while you type. Sometimes words are too long to fit at the end of a line and need to be hyphenated. You can instruct Word to do this for you.

1 Click Page Layout on the Ribbon.

2 Click the Hyphenation button in the Page Layout box to show the drop-down menu.

3 Click the type of hyphenation you want to use in your document (none, automatic or manual).

4 Click Hyphenation Options to fine tune your settings.

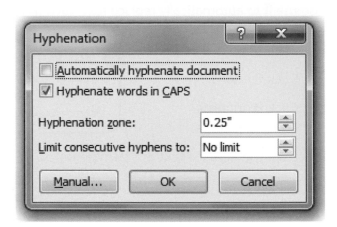

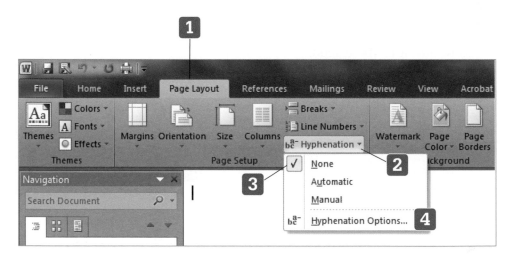

? DID YOU KNOW?
You can use Manual hyphenation to prevent Word from automatically dividing certain words.

🔥 HOT TIP: Do you have too many hyphenated words in a row? Change the Consecutive Hyphens settings in the Hyphenation Options box.

Removing optional hyphens

If you've added hyphenations to your document and don't like the way it looks, you can quickly remove all of those hyphens in one simple step. Just use the Find and Replace function that we discussed before.

1 Click the Home tab on the ribbon.

2 Click Replace in the Editing box.

3 Click the More button in the Replace box.

4 Click the Find box to place your insertion point.

5 Click the Special button and select Optional Hyphen.

6 Leave the Replace box empty because you want to remove the hyphens, not replace them.

7 Click Replace All and all optional hyphens will be removed.

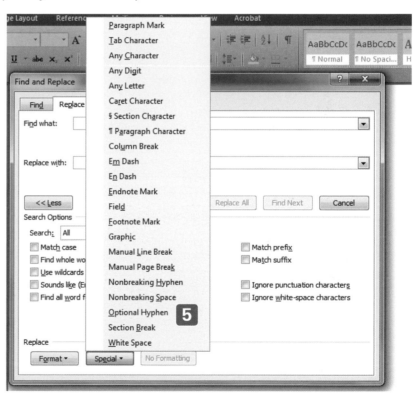

? DID YOU KNOW?
You can use the Format instead of the Special menu to find and replace formatting elements such as fonts and heading styles.

🔥 HOT TIP: You can use this feature to find and remove all types of elements from your documents, including em dashes and graphics.

4 Advanced formatting for Word documents

Introduction

Advanced formatting techniques can help you create professional looking documents. By manipulating your text layout and adding styles, you can easily arrange your content in an organised and easy-to-read format. Choose from Word's pre-set formatting options or customise everything until you find just the right look.

Applying a Quick Style

Microsoft Word provides sets of pre-designed styles that you can use to quickly and easily apply multiple formatting changes to selected text. You can use Styles to create consistent headings or to add emphasis to specific areas of your document.

1 Select the text or word block that you want to format.

2 Click the Home tab on the Ribbon.

3 Place your cursor over the Style in the Styles box that you want to apply.

4 Click the Style to apply it to your document.

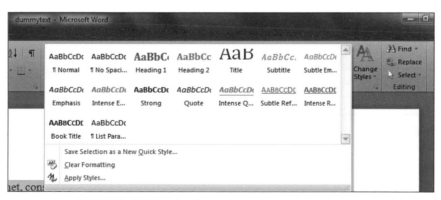

 HOT TIP: Hovering over the various Styles will activate the Live Preview function, allowing you to see what the Style will look like when applied to your document.

 DID YOU KNOW?
You can use the scroll bar in the Styles box to see even more Quick Styles.

Modifying a Quick Style

If one of Word's pre-set Styles doesn't work for your document, you can easily modify the style closest to what you want to suit your needs.

1 Click the Home tab on the Ribbon.

2 Click the arrow in the Styles box to open the Style dialogue.

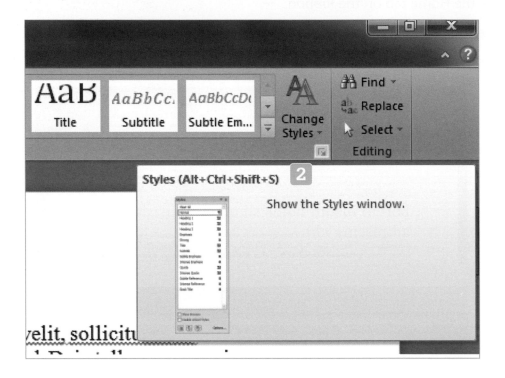

 HOT TIP: Hover your cursor over the Styles in the Style dialogue box to learn more about each style from Word's Screen Tips.

 DID YOU KNOW?

If you modify an existing Word style, any text using that style will change automatically to reflect your adjustments.

3 Right-click the style you wish to change to access the shortcut menu.

4 Click Modify.

5 Make changes to the Style and click OK.

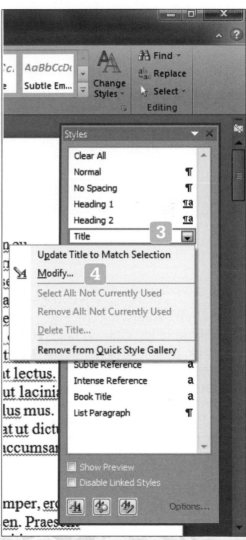

Changing a Style set

The styles that you see in the Style box on the Home tab are only some of the available styles in Word 2010. You can find other style sets in groups such as Modern, Elegant and Professional if you know where to look.

1 Click the Home tab on the Ribbon.

2 Click Change Styles.

3 Position your cursor over Style Set to access the pop-up menu.

4 Click the Style set that you want to change to.

 HOT TIP: You can change your Quick Style default Style set by selecting a new style and then selecting Set as Default from the Change Style menu.

 DID YOU KNOW?

Selecting a new style set applies it to your open document. Use Live Preview to see how it will look before you select it.

Using the Format Painter

By using the Format Painter, you can copy the format from any text and apply it to another selection in your document.

1 Click Home.

2 Select the text block or heading that has the formatting you would like to copy.

3 Click the Format Painter in the Clipboard group on the Home tab.

4 Click-drag your mouse to 'paint' over the text you want to transfer the formatting to.

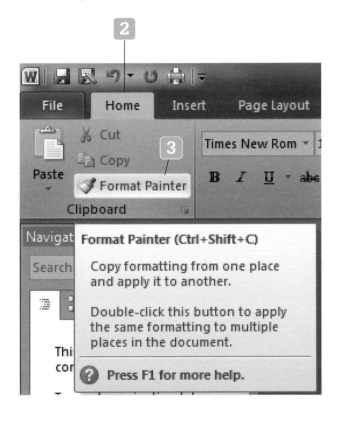

 HOT TIP: You can also use the keyboard shortcut Ctrl-Shift-C to access the Format Painter.

 DID YOU KNOW?
Double-clicking the Format Painter button allows you to apply the copied formatting to multiple areas in your document.

Changing the alignment of text

You can use the Paragraph group on the Home tab to quickly change the alignment of text.

1 Click the Home tab on the Ribbon.

2 Select the text that you want to apply alignment changes to.

3 Click on the alignment button that represents the alignment you want to apply.

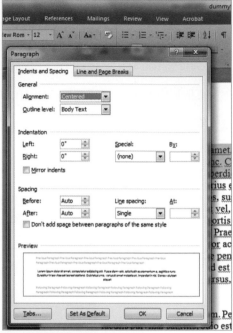

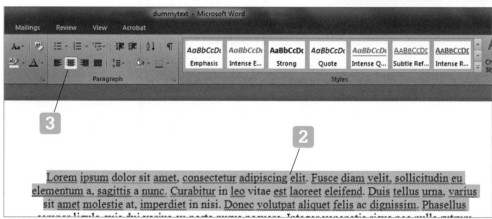

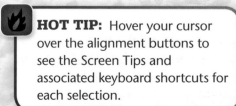

Lorem ipsum dolor sit amet, consectetur adipiscing elit. Fusce diam velit, sollicitudin eu elementum a, sagittis a nunc. Curabitur in leo vitae est laoreet eleifend. Duis tellus urna, varius sit amet molestie at, imperdiet in nisi. Donec volutpat aliquet felis ac dignissim. Phasellus

HOT TIP: Hover your cursor over the alignment buttons to see the Screen Tips and associated keyboard shortcuts for each selection.

DID YOU KNOW?

If you need additional formatting options, click the small arrow to expand the Paragraph Formatting dialogue box.

Adjusting line spacing

The Paragraph group on the Ribbon offers many choices for line spacing within your document.

1 Click the Home tab on the Ribbon.

2 Click the Line and Paragraph Spacing button to see the drop-down menu.

3 Select the spacing you want to use.

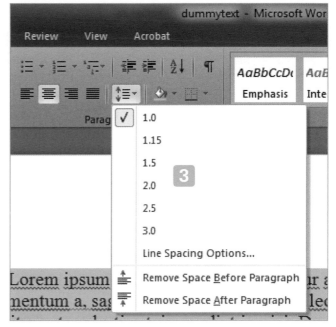

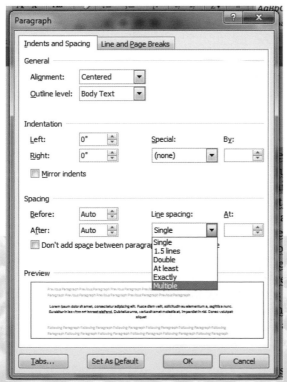

HOT TIP: If you are using a variety of fonts and graphics in your document, try the At Least spacing option. This will arrange your document so that all of the elements fit together.

? DID YOU KNOW?

If you want precise control over your line spacing, use the Multiple setting. You can set this from 0.5 (half of a line space) to as much space as you need.

Increasing and decreasing indents

Some texts require indents at the beginning of each paragraph. Using Word's indentation settings will give you much more control than using the tab key on your keyboard.

1 Place your insertion mark at the beginning or end of the text you want to indent.

2 Click the Home tab on the Ribbon.

3 Click the Increase Indent button in the Paragraph group.

4 Click the Decrease Indent button to undo your change.

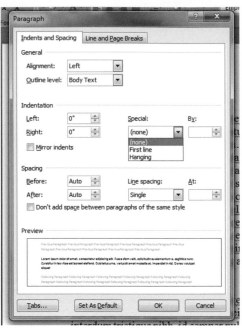

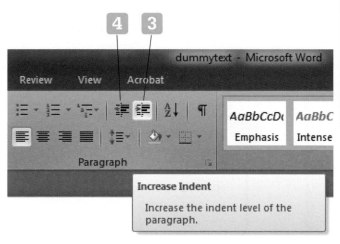

Showing and hiding formatting symbols

Sometimes if your document doesn't quite look right or if you want to make additional changes to your formatting, showing the formatting symbols can help.

1 Click the File tab on the Ribbon.

2 Click Options to access Word Options.

3 Click Display.

4 Click the box next to the formatting symbol you wish to be displayed.

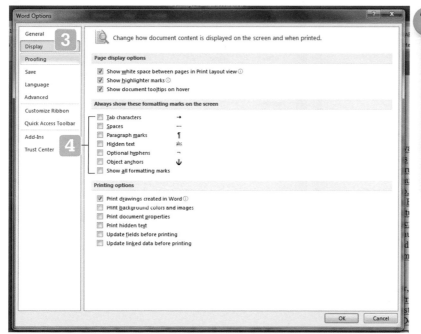

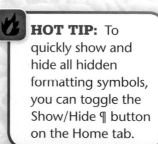

DID YOU KNOW?

Once you've displayed the formatting symbols, they can be manipulated just like regular characters. Cut, copy and paste them as you like.

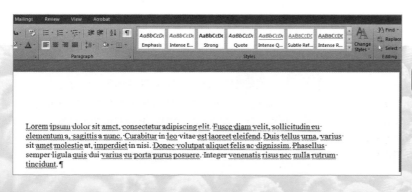

HOT TIP: To quickly show and hide all hidden formatting symbols, you can toggle the Show/Hide ¶ button on the Home tab.

Setting tabs

You can change the settings for your document's tabs by using the Tab options box.

1　Click the Home tab on the Ribbon.

2　Click the arrow in the Paragraph box to expand the Paragraph Settings dialogue box.

3　Click the Tabs button.

4　Change the Tab settings and click OK to apply them.

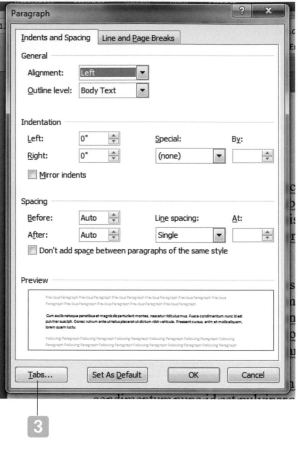

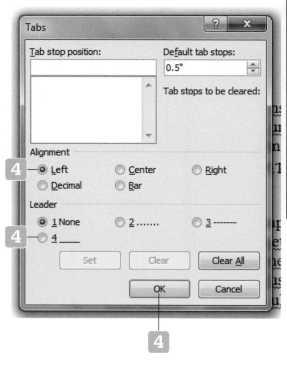

Showing and hiding rulers

Word comes with two rulers (horizontal and vertical) that can be displayed to help you perfectly align text and graphic elements. You can hide and show these rulers as you need them.

1 Click the View tab on the Ribbon.

2 Click the tickbox next to Ruler.

3 Untick the box to hide the ruler again.

HOT TIP: You can also show the ruler by clicking the View Ruler button at the top of your side scroll bar.

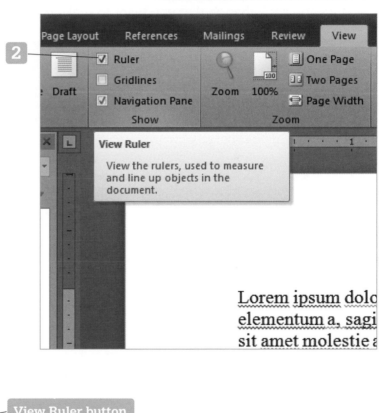

View Ruler button

DID YOU KNOW?

You can change the measurement units that Word uses by clicking on File>Options>Advanced and scrolling down to the Display section.

Changing capitalisation

It's not really that hard to use the Shift or Caps Lock key to add capitalised letters to your words as you type, but Word 2010 has a Change Case function that allows you to apply capitalisation rules to selected text after inputting it.

1 Select the text that you want to add capitalisation to.

2 Click the Home tab on the Ribbon.

3 Click the Change Case button to access the menu.

4 Click the case change that you want to make to apply it to your text.

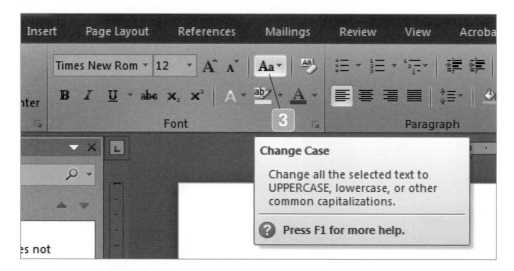

ALERT: If you don't select text before you use the Change Case button, Word will automatically select the word just after your insertion point.

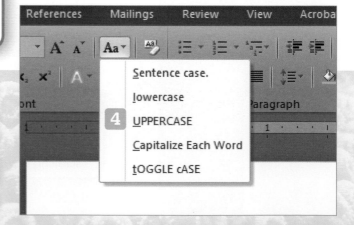

DID YOU KNOW?
Word also allows you to use small caps in words but you won't find that in the Change Case menu. Instead open the Font Settings box and look for it under Effects.

Adding sub- and superscript

Sub- and Superscripts are used most frequently in mathematical equations and scientific formulas but you can add them anywhere in your Word document via the Ribbon.

 1 Click the Home tab on the Ribbon.

2 Select the text that you want to change.

3 Click the Sub- or Superscript box in the Font group.

HOT TIP: You can also change script types in the Font dialogue box, as shown here.

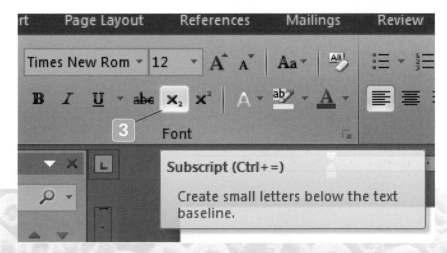

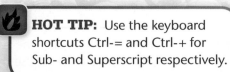 **HOT TIP:** Use the keyboard shortcuts Ctrl-= and Ctrl-+ for Sub- and Superscript respectively.

Using special characters and symbols

You can access the Special Characters menu to add currency symbols, maths symbols, letters with accent marks and more to your Word documents.

1 Click the Insert tab on the Ribbon.

2 Place your insertion point where you want to add your special character.

3 Click Symbol.

4 Click the symbol that you want to add.

> **? DID YOU KNOW?**
> Word keeps track of your most frequently used symbols so you don't have to open the More Symbols menu every time you want to use it.

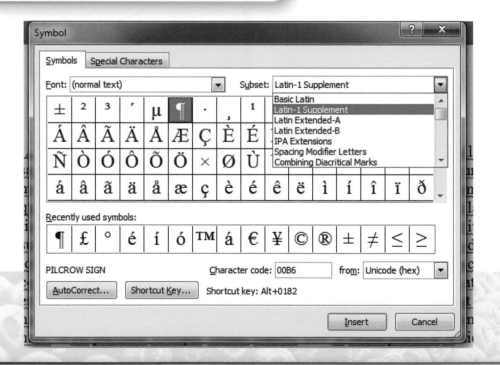

 HOT TIP: If you don't see the symbol or letter you want to add, click More Symbols to see a more complete menu. Use the scroll bar to see all of your choices.

Adding equations

Whether you're a maths teacher or an astrophysicist, you'll appreciate being able to add basic to advanced equations to your Word documents.

1 Click the Insert tab on the Ribbon.

2 Click Equation.

3 Click on a pre-set equation to add it to your document.

4 Click Insert New Equation to build your own.

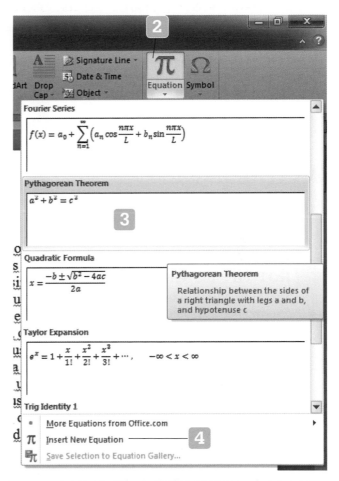

Fourier Series

$$f(x) = a_0 + \sum_{n=1}^{\infty} \left(a_n \cos\frac{n\pi x}{L} + b_n \sin\frac{n\pi x}{L} \right)$$

Pythagorean Theorem

$$a^2 + b^2 = c^2$$

Quadratic Formula

$$x = \frac{-b \pm \sqrt{b^2 - 4ac}}{2a}$$

Pythagorean Theorem

Relationship between the sides of a right triangle with legs a and b, and hypotenuse c

Taylor Expansion

$$e^x = 1 + \frac{x}{1!} + \frac{x^2}{2!} + \frac{x^3}{3!} + \cdots, \quad -\infty < x < \infty$$

Trig Identity 1

More Equations from Office.com

π Insert New Equation

Save Selection to Equation Gallery...

? DID YOU KNOW?

Clicking New Equation or clicking on an equation within your document will give you access to the Equation Tools menu where you can build any equation you need.

? DID YOU KNOW?

You can download more common equations from the Microsoft Office Website.

Formatting fonts

You can add a variety of effects to your text by formatting the font. You'll find the standard formatting options such as bold, italics and underline, but you may be surprised by what else you find.

1 Click the Home tab on the Ribbon.

2 Click the arrow to launch the Font dialogue box.

3 Click the box next to the effect you want to use.

4 Click Text Effects to see more options such as shadow, glow and 3D text.

HOT TIP: You can click the Text Effects button on the Ribbon (Home>Font) to quickly add shadow or glow to selected text.

HOT TIP: When using the Underline Text button on the Ribbon, click the small arrow to access a menu of line styles.

Changing font colours

You can use font colours to call attention to specific areas or words in your document.

1 Click the Home tab on the Ribbon.

2 Click the Text Colour button in the Font group to access the Colour menu.

3 Click the colour you want to use for your text.

4 Click More Colors or Gradient for even more options.

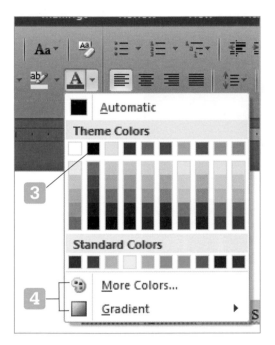

HOT TIP: Use the Custom tab on the More Colours menu to create the perfect colour.

ALERT: Select already coloured text in order to access the Gradient option on the Color menu.

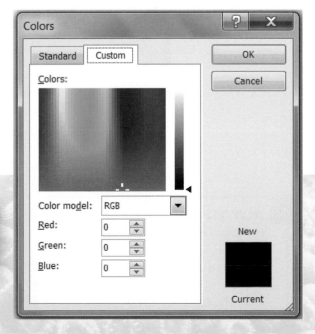

Adding and removing highlighting

Just like using a highlighter pen on a paper document, you can use Word's Highlight feature to highlight text in a variety of colours.

1 Click the Home tab on the Ribbon.

2 Click Text Highlight Color in the Font box.

3 Click the arrow to access additional highlight colours.

4 Click the Text Highlight Color button again to turn highlighting off.

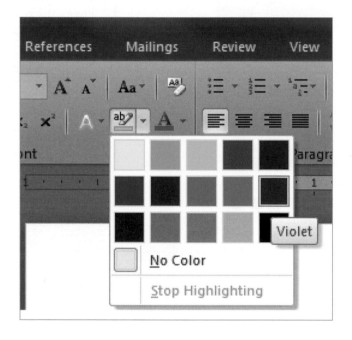

 HOT TIP: You can use selection commands to highlight text blocks. Double-click on a word to highlight the entire word or hold shift and click at the end of a sentence to highlight all of the text.

 DID YOU KNOW?

If you use Highlight Text or any other button a lot, you can right-click on the button to add it to the Quick Access toolbar.

Clearing formatting

Now that you have your document all formatted with special text effects, custom tab stops and a style, what happens when you want it all back the way it was? You can use the Clear Formatting button to strip away all of your settings and go back to plain text.

1 Click the Home tab on the Ribbon.

2 Select the area where you wish to remove the formatting.

3 Click Clear Formatting.

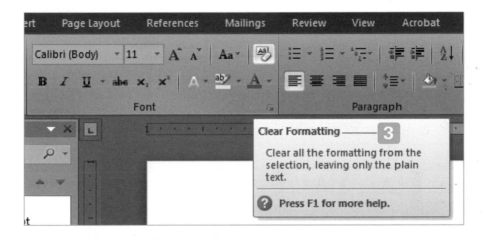

 ALERT: Clear formatting really does clear *all* formatting. Make sure that you really want to return to plain text before you use this function.

 HOT TIP: If you want to return to your formatted text, click Undo immediately after you clear the formatting.

Choosing a theme

You can use a theme to take the guesswork out of selecting complementary elements for your document. A theme includes a variety of colours, each of which is assigned to a particular element. Your theme also includes fonts and effect formatting.

1 Click the Page Layout tab on the Ribbon.

2 Click Themes to activate a drop-down menu.

3 Scroll through the available themes.

4 Click the one that you want to apply it to your document.

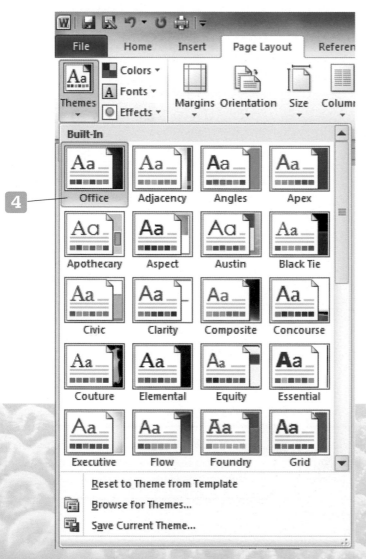

? DID YOU KNOW?
You can personalise a theme by using the Colors, Fonts and Effects drop-down menus to the right of the Themes button.

HOT TIP: You can access many themes for Word online and not just from the Microsoft Office website.

5 Page layout and personalisation

Introduction

When it comes to designing a document, page layout is one of the most important things to consider. Margins, tabs and text layout can make a document easy to read and visually interesting. For professional or scholastic reports, adding resources like a table of contents and bibliography is critical.

Setting page margins

Page margins can help make a document easy to read. Setting wide margins gives a more spacious appearance while narrow margins create a denser look and fit more text. Depending on what kind of document you want to create, you may want to change the margins to something more suitable.

1 Click Page Layout.

2 Click Margins.

3 Click one of the pre-set margins to apply it to your document.

4 Click Custom Margins to set the margins yourself.

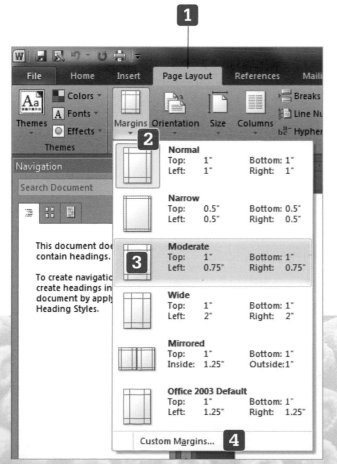

? **DID YOU KNOW?**
If you've set custom margins, your last used settings will appear at the top of the pre-set menu.

! **ALERT:** In the Preview box you can choose to apply your margins to the whole document or from this point forward. If you choose 'This point forward', Word will create a page break and apply your new margins to all text thereafter.

Setting margins for multiple pages

Word has many tools to help you design all types of documents, including two-sided ones like books and catalogues. Setting margins for these types of documents is important, especially if the document is to be bound.

1 Click the Page Layout tab on the Ribbon.

2 Click Margins.

3 Click Custom Margins.

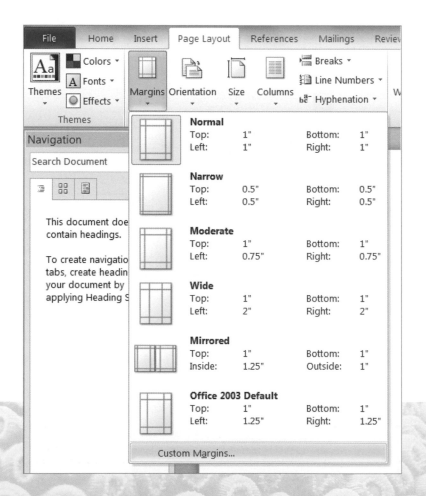

4. Click the drop-down Multiple pages menu under the Pages section.

5. Click the margin style that is most relevant to your project.

6. Click OK to apply the margin style to your document.

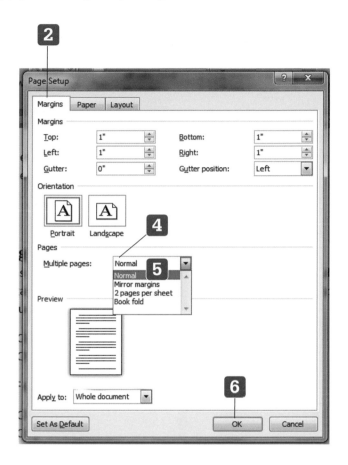

2

Page Setup

Margins | Paper | Layout

Margins

Top: 1"   Bottom: 1"

Left: 1"   Right: 1"

Gutter: 0"   Gutter position: Left

Orientation

Portrait   Landscape

4

Pages

Multiple pages: Normal **5**

Normal
Mirror margins
2 pages per sheet
Book fold

Preview

Apply to: Whole document

6

Set As Default   OK   Cancel

 HOT TIP: Choose Book Fold to print two pages on one sheet. Just fold the paper in half and you have facing pages!

 DID YOU KNOW?

The Gutter setting in the Custom Margins dialogue box refers to the part of the page that is covered with binding.

Changing the page orientation

Most documents are designed in portrait format; that is, the narrow end of the paper is at the top. Sometimes it's better to design a wider document when you have more horizontal content, so you can use the landscape page orientation to do so.

1 Click Page Layout.

2 Click Orientation.

3 Click Portrait or Landscape to apply the change to your document.

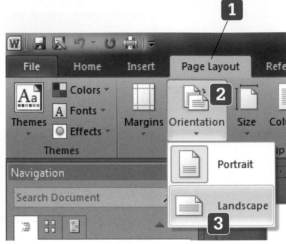

? DID YOU KNOW?

You can also change the page orientation in the Page Layout settings. Just click on Page Layout>Margins>Custom Margins to open the dialogue box.

Inserting headers and footers

Headers and footers are handy to have in documents. You can add information that appears across multiple pages throughout a document, such as page numbers, the document title, the author's name or the date it was created.

1 Click the Insert tab on the Ribbon.

2 Click either Header or Footer to see a drop-down menu.

3 Use the scroll bar to see the Header and Footer style options.

4 Click the style that you want to add, to apply it to your document.

5 Click the text boxes and replace the dummy text with your customisations.

6 Click Close Header and Footer to save your changes.

2

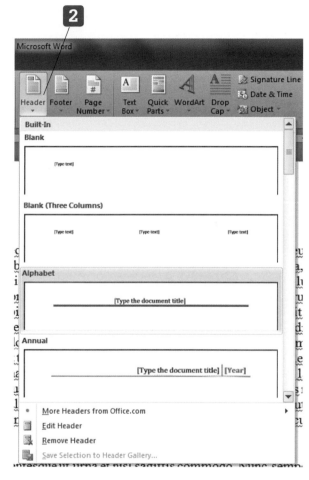

> **HOT TIP:** Find more Header and Footer styles online at the Microsoft Office website.

> **? DID YOU KNOW?**
> There's a matching footer style for every header style. For style consistency, use them together.

6

5

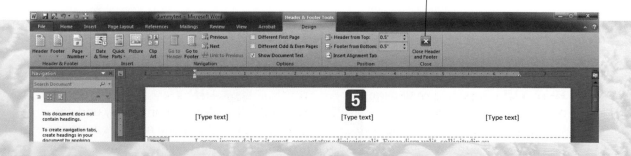

Adding and removing page numbers

You don't have to open the Header and Footer tools to add page numbers to your document. You can just use the Page Number button on the Ribbon and select from the options.

1 Click the Insert tab on the Ribbon.

2 Click Page Number in the Header & Footer box to open the drop-down menu.

3 Click the page number style that appeals to you to select it.

4 Click Close Header and Footer to save your changes.

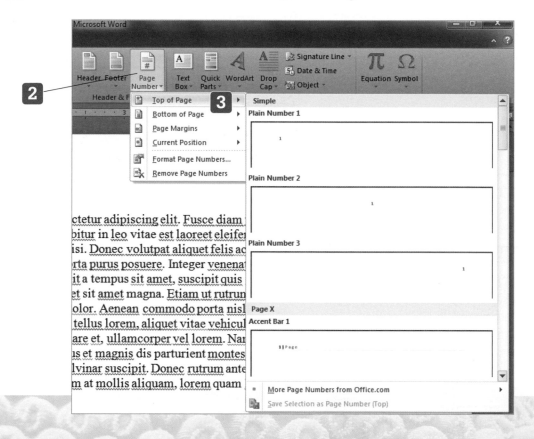

HOT TIP: To remove your page numbers, just open the Page Number drop-down menu and click Remove Page Numbers.

DID YOU KNOW?
Word automatically updates your page numbers as your document grows.

Adding columns

Columns are especially helpful when designing newsletters and reports. They add a nice visual element to a document by breaking up large expanses of text and making them easier to read.

1 Click Page Layout.

2 Click the Columns button to see the drop-down menu.

3 Select the number of columns that you want to use.

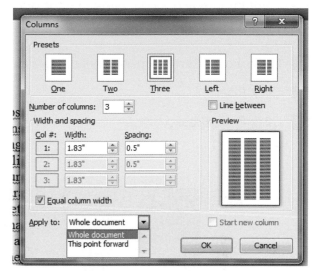

HOT TIP: If you want to customise your columns layout, select More Columns from the drop-down menu.

? DID YOU KNOW?

Just as with margins, you can select to apply your new columns to the whole document or just from this point forward.

Adding a page break

Adding a page break is a great way to divide a long document into sections. A page break ends the page immediately. This provides a better method than simply hitting enter until you reach a new page in your document, which can sometimes create formatting problems.

1 Place your insertion mark where you want to create a page break.

2 Click Insert.

3 Click Page Break.

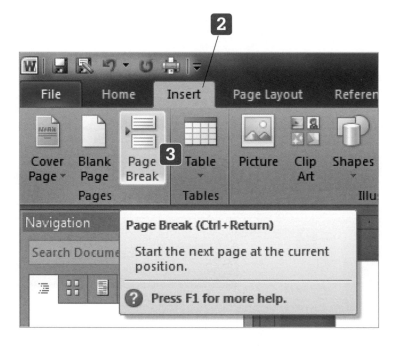

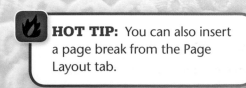

HOT TIP: You can also insert a page break from the Page Layout tab.

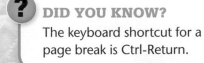

DID YOU KNOW?
The keyboard shortcut for a page break is Ctrl-Return.

Adding a section break

You can use section breaks to make formatting changes to a specified section of your document. For example, you can insert a section of pages that are in landscape format into a document that's using portrait orientation or you could create just a section in a report that uses multiple columns.

1 Click Page Layout.

2 Click Breaks to access the drop-down menu.

3 Click the section break that you want to insert.

? DID YOU KNOW?

Next Page section breaks create a new page for your new section while the Continuous section break starts at your insertion point.

Adding bookmarks

Bookmarks can help you or your readers navigate through long documents. Bookmarks don't show up when you print a document but they do allow you to jump directly to a word or paragraph anywhere in your document quickly by using the Navigation pane.

1 Select the word or text block that you want to bookmark.

2 Click the Insert tab on the Ribbon.

3 Click Bookmark in the Links group.

4 Type the name of your bookmark.

5 Click Add.

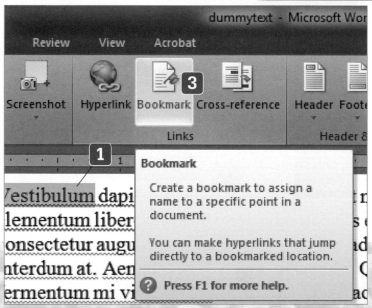

? DID YOU KNOW?
You don't need to select anything to add a bookmark but it makes remembering why you bookmarked it a lot easier later.

 ALERT: Word's default setting is that bookmarks are hidden. To view your bookmarks, click File>Options>Advanced and click Show Bookmarks in the Show Document Content section.

Using bookmarks

Now that you've created bookmarks in your document, you need to know how to access them. You can easily jump to any bookmark in your document with just a few clicks.

1. Click the Home tab on the Ribbon.

2. Click Find to access the drop-down menu.

3. Click Go To.

4. Click Bookmark.

5. Type in the bookmark name or select it from the drop-down menu.

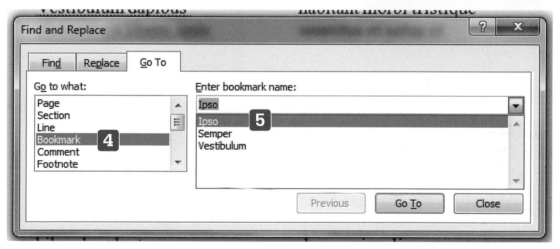

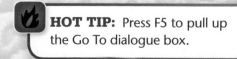 **HOT TIP:** Press F5 to pull up the Go To dialogue box.

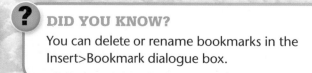 **DID YOU KNOW?**
You can delete or rename bookmarks in the Insert>Bookmark dialogue box.

Creating an index

An index is a list of key words or topics used in your document and what pages they can be found on. Adding an index to a lengthy report provides a helpful and professional touch.

1 Click the References tab on the Ribbon.

2 Select a word in your document that you want to appear in the index.

3 Click Mark Entry in the Index group.

4 Fill in any additional information that you want to add to your index entry and click Mark.

5 Click Insert Index to create an index of all of your marked content.

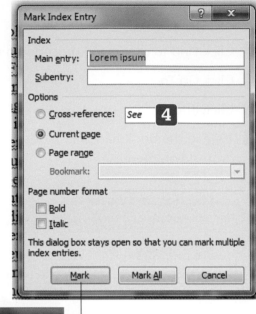

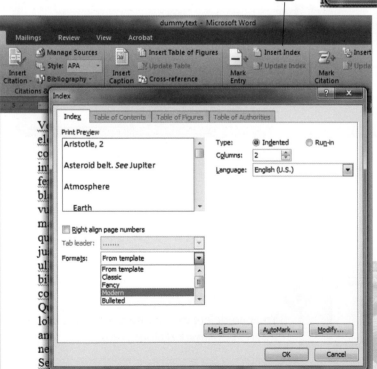

Creating a table of contents

Similar to an index, a table of contents is critical when preparing long documents or reports. Word will build you a table of contents based on your document's content or you can manually create one yourself.

1 Click References.

2 Click Table of Contents to access the drop-down menu.

3 Click the Table that you want to add to your document.

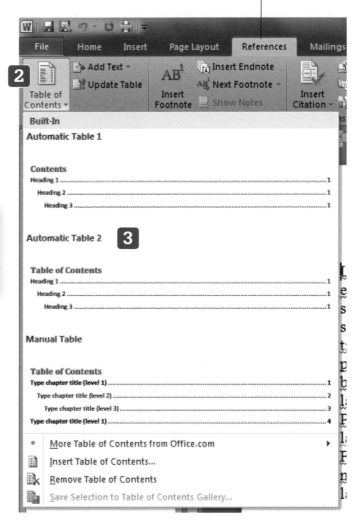

> **HOT TIP:** Once you've added a Table of Contents to your document, use the Add Text to add more chapters or sections.

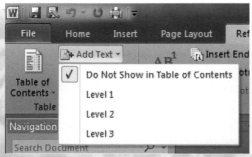

> **ALERT:** Once you've completed your document, make sure to click Update Table to ensure that your Table of Contents lists the page numbers correctly.

Creating a bibliography

You can use Word's Insert Citation function to keep track of your sources as you build your document. Once you've completed your text, you can pull it all together into a perfectly formatted bibliography.

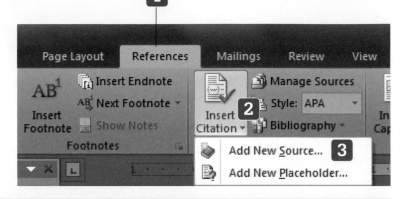

1 Click References.

2 Click the Insert Citation button to add a reference source.

3 Select a citation Style from the drop-down menu.

4 Click Bibliography to choose between Works Cited and Bibliography format.

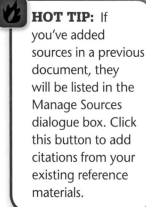 **HOT TIP:** If you've added sources in a previous document, they will be listed in the Manage Sources dialogue box. Click this button to add citations from your existing reference materials.

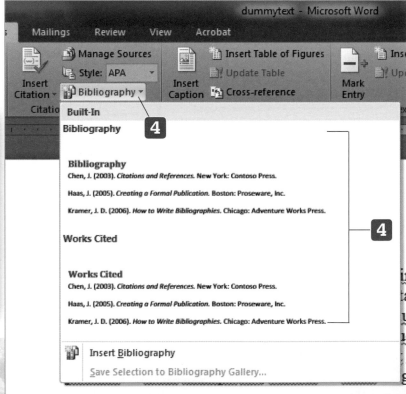

 **DID YOU KNOW?**

If you aren't sure what resource you want to add to a section in your text, click Insert Citation and Add a New Placeholder to remind yourself to add a citation later.

Using text boxes

Text boxes are a great way to highlight quotes in a document. If you are designing a newsletter, you can use text boxes to add sidebars to your work. These boxes help break up dense text and draw the reader's focus to important information.

1 Click the Insert tab on the Ribbon.

2 Click Text Box.

3 Click on a built-in text box style or on Draw Text Box to design your own.

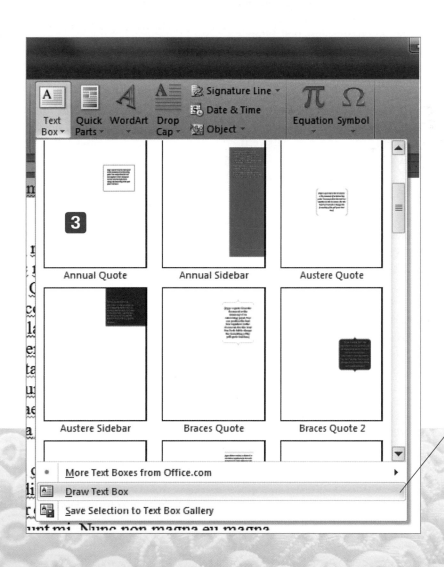

4 Fill in the sample text with your personalised information.

Changing the document background colour

Changing the background colour of your document isn't a very good idea if you are planning on printing it. You should use colour paper instead. However, if you plan to create a document that will be shared electronically, you can change the background to any colour you like.

1 Click the Page Layout tab on the Ribbon.

2 Click Page Color in the Page Background group.

3 Click a colour associated with your document theme or click More Colours.

4 Click Fill Effects to add a photo or texture as your background.

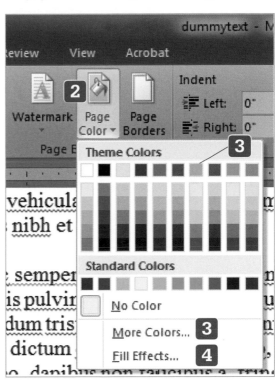

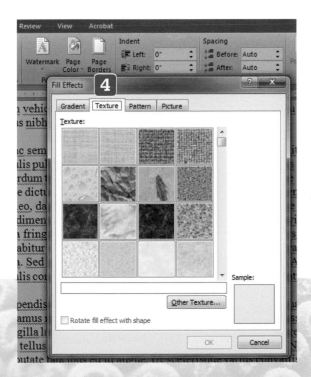

ALERT: Garish backgrounds and bright colours can appear unprofessional and make text hard to read. Use these design elements carefully!

DID YOU KNOW?

You'll need to turn on the Print Background Colors option in the Advanced Word Options menu if you want your backgrounds to be included when printing.

6 Printing and mail merge

Introduction

Some documents will only ever exist in an electronic format, but there's no escaping the printed page. Word offers a variety of print settings to make printing different types of documents easy. You can also use the Mail Merge feature for mailing lists and newsletters.

Using Print Preview

Print Preview does exactly what it sounds like it does; it shows you a preview of what your document will look like when printed. You can use this feature to see how certain design elements look on paper or to check the overall layout of your page.

1 Click View.

2 Click Print Layout from the Document Views group.

3 Click One Page or Two Pages in the Zoom group.

4 Click Page Width to return to your normal view.

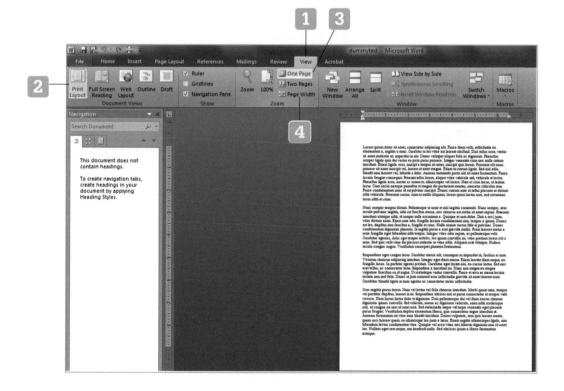

DID YOU KNOW?

You'll also find a Print Preview view in the Print dialogue box.

Adding a printer

It's not uncommon to have more than one printer available to print from, especially if you travel with a laptop. Occasionally, you might print to a file without even using an actual printer. Either way, you'll need to make sure that Word recognises where you want to send your document.

1 Click File.

2 Click Print.

3 Click the drop-down menu under Printer in the Print dialogue to the right.

4 Check if your printer is already listed in the available printers.

5 Click Add Printer to add a new printer to the list.

6 Browse for your printer and click OK.

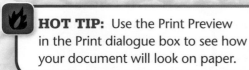 **HOT TIP:** Use the Print Preview in the Print dialogue box to see how your document will look on paper.

? DID YOU KNOW?

If you want to print to a file instead of to a printer, use the drop-down Printer list and select Print to File. Select it again to turn Print to File off.

Printing a document

Now that you know what your document is going to look like and you've set up your printer, it's time to put that text onto real paper! There are several ways that you can print documents from within Word 2010.

1 Click File and click Print.

2 Use the Ctrl-P keyboard shortcut.

3 Click the Print icon on the Quick Access Menu.

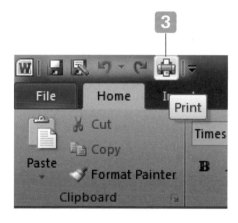

 HOT TIP: Use Quick Print if you only want to print one copy of your document. You'll need to use the Print dialogue box if you want to print multiple copies.

? DID YOU KNOW?

If you want to change your default printer in Word, you'll need to change it in your computer's system settings first.

Printing to a file

You can print your document to a file for safekeeping or to take the file to a commercial printer.

1 Click File.

2 Click Print.

3 Click Printer to access the Printer list.

4 Scroll to the bottom of the list and click Print to File.

5 Click Print.

6 Name your document and choose a Save location in the resulting window.

7 Click OK to save and exit.

DID YOU KNOW?
When you print to a file, Word saves the formatting information of your document so it will look the same when it's printed on paper.

ALERT: Make sure you can remember where you've saved your documents to. It makes sense to save them all in one location, like My Documents, for example.

Printing to PDF

PDF is one of the most popular file formats for sending readable materials. It has a good compression ratio so even large documents can be sent electronically and anyone can read them by using the free Adobe Reader available for download on Adobe's website.

1 Click File.

2 Click Print.

3 Click Printer to access the Printer list.

4 Click Adobe PDF.

5 Click Print.

6 Name your document and choose a Save location in the resulting window.

7 Click OK to save and exit.

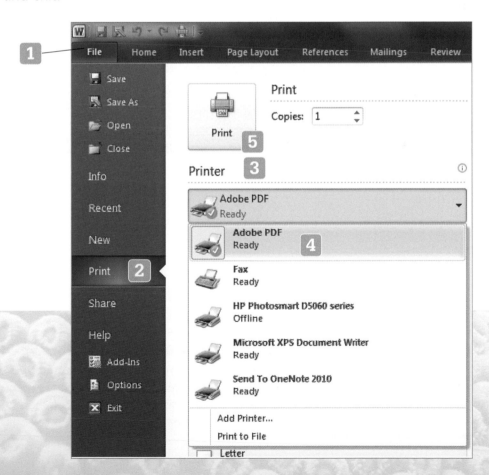

Cancelling a print job

How you cancel a print job is determined by whether or not you have Background Printing turned on in your Advanced Word Options. When you print in the background, you can continue to work while your document is being printed. If you don't, you'll be able to see your printing status and cancel printing by clicking cancel.

1 Double-click the printer icon in your operating system's status bar.

2 Right-click the document you want to cancel.

3 Click Cancel to cancel printing.

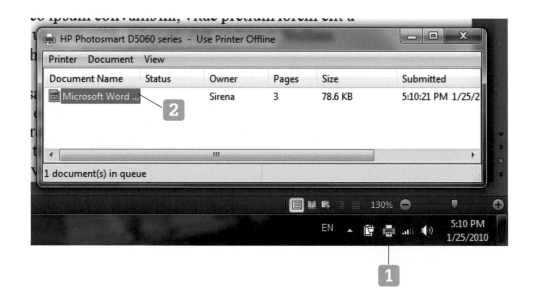

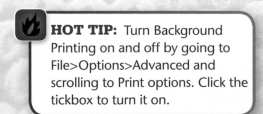

HOT TIP: Turn Background Printing on and off by going to File>Options>Advanced and scrolling to Print options. Click the tickbox to turn it on.

? DID YOU KNOW?
You can pause or restart your print job from the same menu as cancelling your print job.

Changing the print quality

If you've had your printer long, you probably know how expensive replacement ink cartridges are! Well, if you want to conserve ink, try printing your documents at a lower quality. You can set the quality to use less ink or to only print in black and white.

1 Click File.

2 Click Print.

3 Click Printer Properties under the Printer button.

4 Select a new print quality from the drop-down menu.

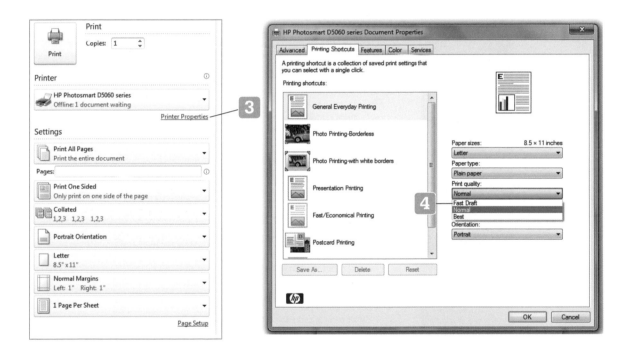

 HOT TIP: Use the Fast Draft setting for casual documents and save the Best setting for photos or graphics-heavy documents.

 DID YOU KNOW?

Depending on your printer, you may have Printing shortcuts that offer more quality settings than just the standard three (Draft, Normal and Best).

Printing specific pages

Sometimes it's best just to print a page or two instead of an entire document. You can set the page range in Word to print only even, only odd or you can specify pages one by one.

1 Click File.

2 Click Print.

3 Click Print All Pages, under Settings.

4 Click Print Custom Range to select pages to print or select another option from the list.

 ALERT: You'll find options to print only odd or even pages at the very end of the Print All Pages menu.

 HOT TIP: When entering a custom page range, you can add individual pages separated by commas or use a hyphen to set a range of pages (10-23, for example).

Printing and collating multiple copies

It's a good idea to use the Collate feature when you are printing multiple copies of a multi-page document. This keeps the pages in order and the copies as a unit.

1 Click File.

2 Click Print.

3 Click Collated and select the type of collating that you want.

4 Click the box where it says Copies and enter a number or use the arrows to increase/decrease the number of copies you want.

5 Click Print.

ALERT: If you don't select a collation setting, Word will print all of the copies of each page as a group by default.

HOT TIP: Use Ctrl-P to open the Print dialogue box.

Printing a landscape document

Using the Portrait Orientation button in the Print dialogue box will allow you to change your document from Portrait to Landscape when you print.

1 Click File.

2 Click Print.

3 Click Portrait Orientation.

4 Click the layout that you want, portrait or landscape.

5 Click the Print button at the top of the page.

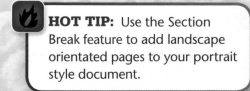 **HOT TIP:** Use the Section Break feature to add landscape orientated pages to your portrait style document.

DID YOU KNOW?

If you've already set up your page layout to landscape, you won't need to change your settings in the print dialogue.

Printing a two-sided document

Printing on both sides of the page is not just space-saving, but paper-saving too. Two-sided printing is standard for booklets and other bound materials.

1 Click File.

2 Click Print.

3 Click Print One Sided to access the drop-down menu.

4 Select how you would like your document printed from the available options.

5 Click Print at the top of the page.

 ALERT: You need a printer capable of printing two-sided documents to use this feature, otherwise select Manually Print on Both Sides. This will prompt you to flip over the paper and reload it into the printer.

 HOT TIP: Print draft copies of the first couple of pages of your document. You'll need to determine which direction to insert the paper back into the printer for the second side to print on the correct page.

Printing an envelope

Most printers come with an envelope tray that fits standard envelope sizes. You should refer to the instructions that came with your printer to determine how to load the envelopes properly before printing.

1 Click the Mailings tab on the Ribbon.

2 Click Envelopes in the Create group.

3 Enter the address in the text box or use the add Microsoft Outlook Contact button.

4 Add your return address or select Omit if using pre-printed envelopes.

5 Click Options to see additional envelope sizes and other settings.

6 Click OK to save your options.

7 Click Print to print your envelopes.

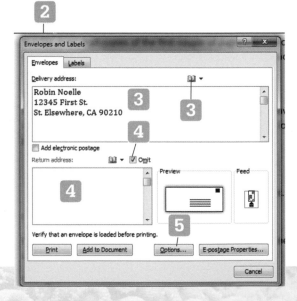

? DID YOU KNOW?

You can change the feed options by clicking on the Printing Options tab in the Options box.

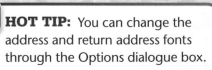

🔥 HOT TIP: You can change the address and return address fonts through the Options dialogue box.

Printing a label

Word has the capability to help you design labels based on a wide variety of standard label sizes. There are settings that are specific to certain manufacturers and style numbers. These steps will help you print a single label from a sheet.

1 Click the Mailings tab on the Ribbon.

2 Click Labels in the Create group.

3 Click Options.

 ALERT: Check to make sure that your label sheet is loaded into the printer properly so you don't print on the wrong side.

4 Select the label vendor from the drop-down menu.

5 Select your label style from the resulting list.

6 Select OK.

7 Click Single Label to select printing only one label from a sheet.

8 Use the arrows to set the row and column of the label you want to print.

9 Click Print.

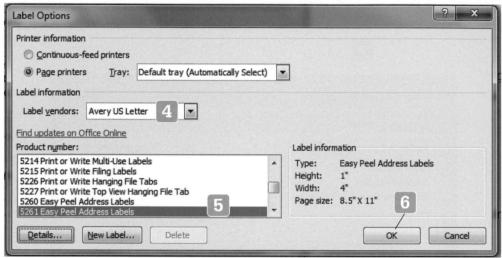

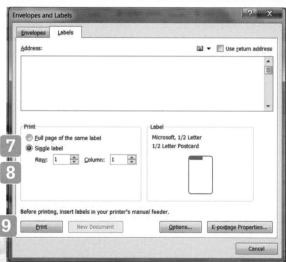

HOT TIP: Click Full Page of Same labels if you want to print a whole page of duplicates.

? DID YOU KNOW?

If you have e-postage software on your computer, you can print postage on labels or envelopes through Word.

Creating a form letter using Mail Merge

You can use Mail Merge to create documents meant to be sent to a large group of people using a data source like a mailing list. You can easily create form letters that will be populated by the information in these lists.

1 Click the Mailings tab on the Ribbon.

2 Click Start Mail Merge.

3 Select Letters.

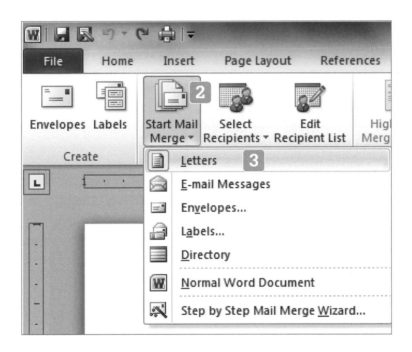

? **DID YOU KNOW?**

You can also use the Step by Step Mail Merge wizard to quickly create mail merge documents such as labels, envelopes, catalogues and more.

4 Click Select Recipients to attach your letter to a data source like an Excel spreadsheet or Outlook address book.

5 Type your letter and add fields from the Write & Insert Fields group on the Ribbon.

6 Click Preview Results to see how your letter will look.

7 Click Finish & Merge to complete your letter and save it to your hard drive.

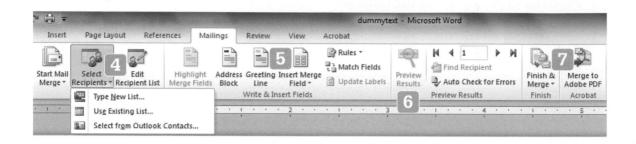

HOT TIP: Want to eliminate some of the people on your mailing list? Just use Edit Recipient List to add or remove contacts.

7 Graphics and photos

Introduction

You can really add some personal style to your documents by adding graphics and photos. Design a family newsletter using your favourite photos or add a SmartArt chart to spice up a corporate report. Graphics make your documents more visually interesting and enjoyable to read. Word 2010 makes working with image files a breeze!

Finding clip art

Clip art is a collection of royalty-free images that you can use in your document. Most often the images are illustrations or drawings. Microsoft Office has made clip art available in Word and also online.

1 Click the Insert tab on the Ribbon.

2 Click Clip Art in the Illustrations group.

3 Type a keyword that relates to the subject of the desired graphic in the Search for text box.

4 Select the type of media files you want to search for from the drop-down menu.

5 Click Go.

HOT TIP: If you click the Include Office.com content tickbox, Word will check the website for related graphics that you can download. You'll get a lot more results from your search when this option is selected.

? DID YOU KNOW?

You can find hundreds of websites online devoted to free clip art. Just do a search from your favourite search engine and check them out!

Adding clip art to your documents

Now that you know where to find it, it's time to learn how to add clip art to your document.

1 Click the Insert tab on the Ribbon.

2 Click Clip Art in the Illustrations group.

3 Type a keyword that relates to the subject of the desired graphic in the Search for text box.

4 Select the type of media files you want to search for from the drop-down menu.

5 Click Go.

6 Click on the graphic that you want to add.

7 Click-hold on the clip art to position it in your document.

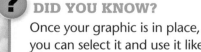

HOT TIP: Look for the arrow that appears on the clip art when your cursor gets close. Click on this arrow to access a menu for that graphic.

? **DID YOU KNOW?**

Once your graphic is in place, you can select it and use it like text. You can cut, copy and paste it into other areas of your document.

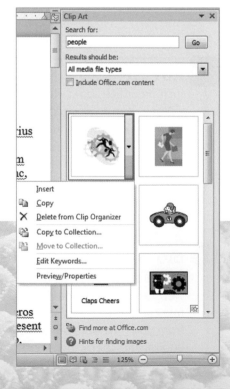

Adding clip art to the Clip Organizer

If you download clip art from the Office.com website, it is automatically stored in the Clip Organizer. If you want to add clip art you've downloaded from other websites or created yourself, you can add those files to your clip organizer to keep them all together.

1 Click the Start button in Windows.

2 Type Clip Organizer in the search bar.

3 Click the Microsoft Clip Organizer icon under Programs to launch the organiser.

4 Click File.

5 Click Add Clips to Organizer.

6 Click On My Own.

7 Browse for the file you want to add, select it and hit OK.

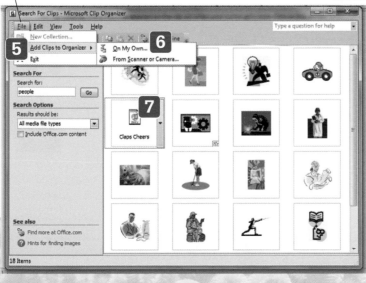

HOT TIP: When your clip is uploaded, use the drop-down menu to edit the keywords associated with the picture. This will make it easy to find when you are searching.

? DID YOU KNOW?

It's not just photos and drawings that are included in your Office.com clip art. There are audio and animated files too.

Downloading clip art from Office.com

Microsoft has a lot of clip art available for Office users. You can download these graphics for free and add them into your clip organiser for later use.

1 Click the Insert tab on the Ribbon.

2 Click Clip Art.

3 Click Find More at Office. com from the resulting search box.

4 Wait for your browser window to open and the website to load.

5 Click the category that you want to view.

6 Click the image that you want to download.

7 Click Download.

8 Browse to a location on your computer where you want to save the file and click OK.

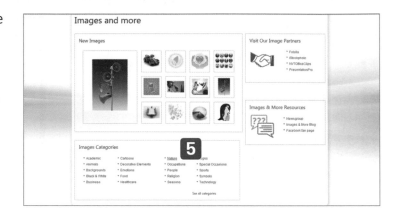

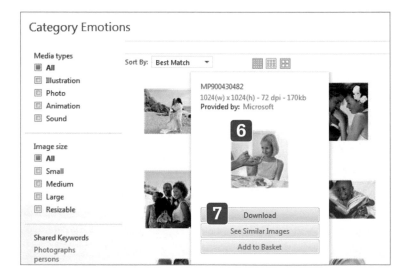

ALERT: If the Save box doesn't appear when you download the file, the image will appear in your browser instead. Right-click on the image and select Save Image As.

DID YOU KNOW?

If you want to download more than one image, add it to your basket. When you've added the clips you want, you can download them all at once.

Adding SmartArt graphics

SmartArt is a collection of graphics designed to convey information, such as organisational charts, Venn diagrams and cycles. You can select a graphic from the list and then fill in the information you wish to convey.

1 Click the Insert tab on the Ribbon.

2 Click SmartArt.

3 Click the category of graphic that you want to view.

4 Click the graphic that you want to add.

5 Click OK to add it to your document.

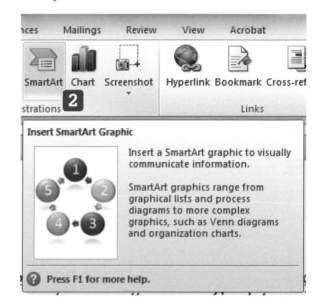

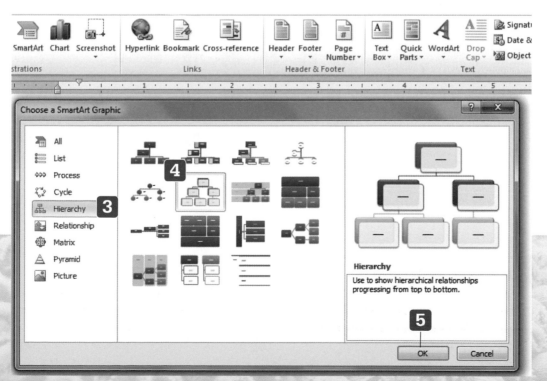

Customising SmartArt graphics

Once you've added the SmartArt graphic to your document, you can customise it with new colours, new text and even change the layout.

1 Click the SmartArt graphic to open the Design menu.

2 Click another layout if you want one from the same group.

3 Type your content in the text box that says Type your text here.

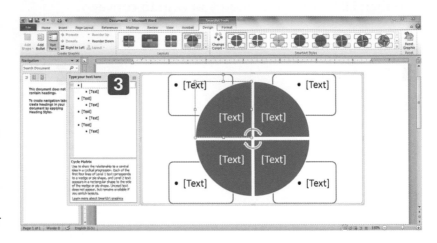

4 Click Change Colors.

5 Scroll through the available colour options or colour it yourself.

6 Click the colour layout that you want to apply.

7 Click a Style from the Styles menu to change the style of your graphic.

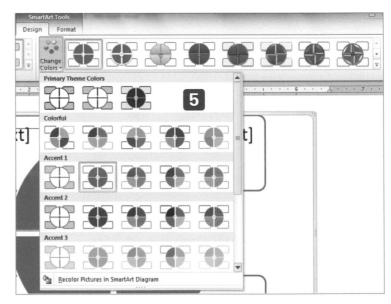

HOT TIP: If you scroll through the available styles, you will find some are 3D!

? DID YOU KNOW?
You can click Reset Graphic to undo all of the formatting changes you've made.

Positioning graphics

The chances are that you won't want to leave an inserted graphic where Word put it. In a few simple steps, you can move your image to where you want it.

1 Click the Insert tab on the Ribbon.

2 Click Clip Art.

3 Search for the art that you want to add.

4 Click the image that you want to add.

5 Click-drag on the image to position it within your text.

6 Click Wrap Text in the Picture Tools toolbar on the Ribbon.

7 Select a text wrapping option from the drop-down menu.

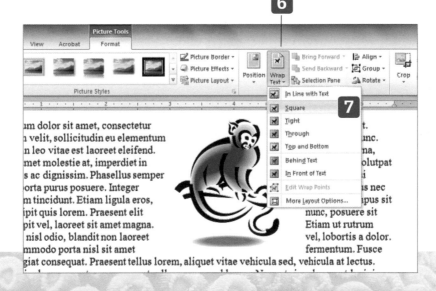

🔥 **HOT TIP:** Use the other buttons in the Arrange group to rotate your image or change the alignment.

❓ **DID YOU KNOW?**

You can replace some of the images in the SmartArt diagrams. Experiment with the Picture Styles buttons to see how it all works.

Resizing graphics

Not all graphics are the same size. You'll probably have to resize most of the images that you add to your documents. Luckily, Word makes this easy.

1 Click on the inserted image in your document to select it.

2 Click-hold one of the small circles in the corners or squares on the sides of the image.

3 Drag the small circle to resize the graphic.

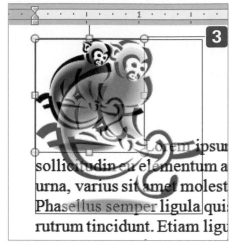

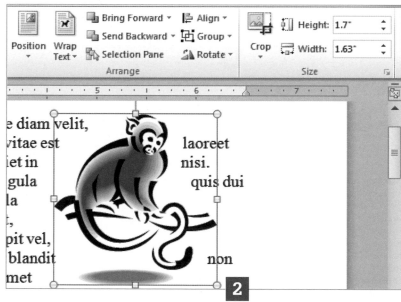

Cropping an image

Sometimes you don't need an entire image in your document, just a small part of it. The screenshots in this book are a good example. You can use the editing features of Word to crop your graphic and only keep a portion of the original image.

1 Click the image you've added to your document to open the Picture Tools toolbar.

2 Click Crop in the Size group.

3 Click-drag a black corner mark to create the size of your cropped image.

4 Click-drag the image until only the part you want visible is in your crop box.

5 Click Crop again to finish cropping.

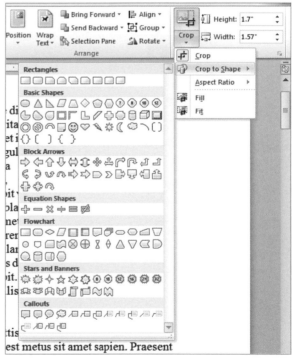

HOT TIP: Click on the arrow in the Crop button to display more cropping options. Here you will find the ability to crop your image into different shapes.

HOT TIP: You can set the Aspect Ratio for your image from the Crop drop-down menu.

Inserting a screenshot

You can insert screenshots of other Word documents or open programs on your computer into your text by using the Screenshot button.

1 Click the Insert tab on the Ribbon.

2 Click Screenshot to open the drop-down menu.

3 Select one of the available windows to insert a copy into your document.

4 Use the Picture Tools to resize and format the resulting screenshot.

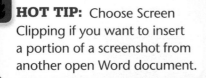 **HOT TIP:** Choose Screen Clipping if you want to insert a portion of a screenshot from another open Word document.

 **DID YOU KNOW?**

You can add a hyperlink to any image in your document. Just right-click on the image and select Add Hyperlink from the menu.

Working with auto shapes

Word 2010 provides you with a set of pre-made shapes that you can add to your document. Once you select your shape, you can change the colour, the size and even add animation.

1 Click Insert.

2 Click Shapes to access the drop-down menu.

3 Click the shape that you would like to add.

4 Drag the crosshairs to create the shape size that you want.

5 Click Shape Styles to change the colour and style of your shape.

HOT TIP: Click on Shape Effects to add cool effects like 3D animation or a neon glow to your shapes.

HOT TIP: If you don't want a specific style, you can always change the colour of your shape via the Shape Fill button in the Shape Style group.

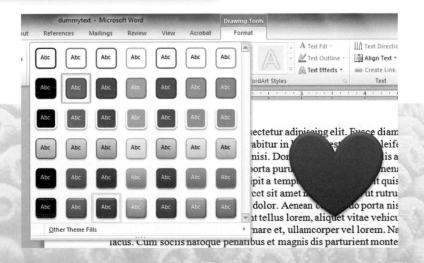

Showing and hiding gridlines

Positioning graphics and photos is a lot easier when you can view the gridlines on your page.

1 Click View.

2 Click Gridlines in the Show group.

3 Click it again to turn them off.

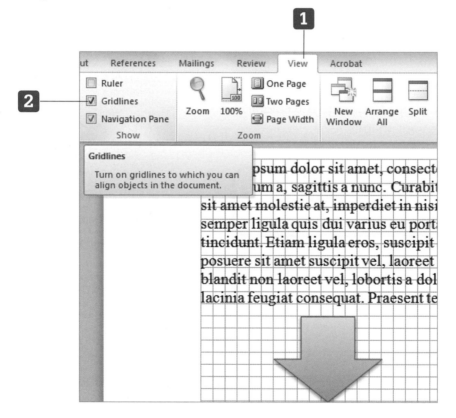

Adding a photo

You can add personal photos to your documents. Use them for 'Lost & Found' posters, event fliers and family newsletters.

1 Click the Insert tab on the Ribbon.

2 Click Picture in the Illustrations group.

3 Browse to your photo directory and select a photo.

4 Click OK to insert it into the text.

5 Resize and place the photo into the desired location.

ALERT: Word may resize your photo when you insert it if it's high resolution. This is because Word imbeds your picture into the file, making it larger. The larger your photo file size is, the larger your Word file becomes.

DID YOU KNOW?
You can use the Picture Tools on your photos too. Use the other tools to add a shape or crop your image.

How to apply a Picture Style

You can radically change the look of your photos by applying a quick Picture Style.

1 Click the graphic that you added or add a graphic to open the Picture Tools toolbar.

2 Click the arrow next to the Picture Styles to expand the menu.

3 Select one of the styles to apply to your photo.

4 Click one of the other Picture Styles buttons to apply more effects.

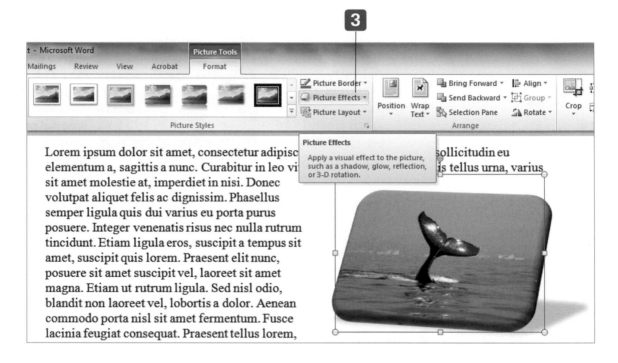

 DID YOU KNOW?
You can use the other Picture Styles effects on your photos, like adding a shadow, contour or colour border.

 HOT TIP: Adding Picture Styles and effects can make your photos look more professional than just inserting and aligning them.

Adding captions

Once you've put your photos in place, you can add captions to tell your readers a little more about them.

1 Right-click on your image to display an additional menu.

2 Click Insert Caption.

3 Type your caption in the appropriate text box.

4 Click OK to add the caption to the photo.

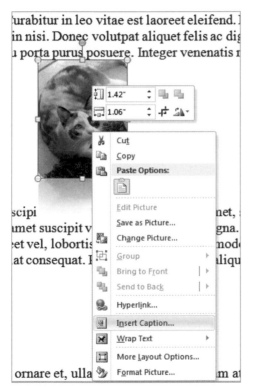

Figure 1: Grace O'Malley

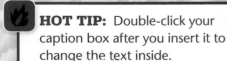

HOT TIP: Double-click your caption box after you insert it to change the text inside.

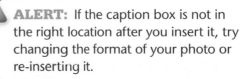

ALERT: If the caption box is not in the right location after you insert it, try changing the format of your photo or re-inserting it.

Adding borders to documents

In Word 2010, you can add a snappy border around any page with just a click of a button.

1 Click the Page Layout tab in the Ribbon.

2 Click Page Borders in the Page Background group.

3 Adjust the settings in the Page Border dialogue box.

4 Click OK to apply the border to your document.

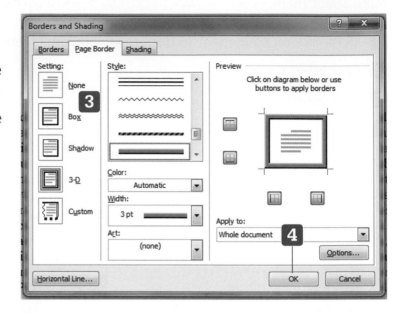

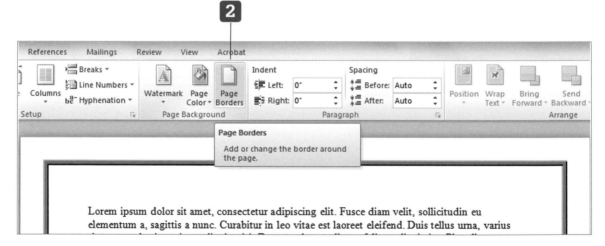

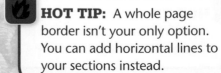

? DID YOU KNOW?
You can also change the border colour or add border art from the Page Border dialogue box.

🔥 HOT TIP: A whole page border isn't your only option. You can add horizontal lines to your sections instead.

Adding and deleting WordArt

If you're looking for a subtle heading for your next business report, try adding WordArt!
Just kidding! WordArt isn't subtle at all. It's bold and exciting!

1 Click the Insert tab on the Ribbon.

2 Select the text that
you want WordArt to
use.

3 Click WordArt.

4 Select a WordArt
style from the
resulting menu.

5 Click OK to insert
your WordArt.

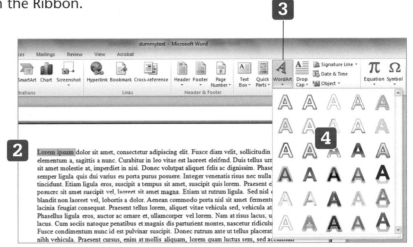

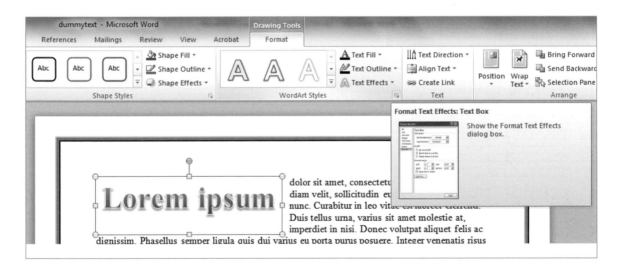

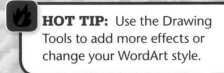 **HOT TIP:** Use the Drawing
Tools to add more effects or
change your WordArt style.

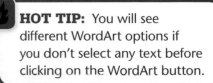 **HOT TIP:** You will see
different WordArt options if
you don't select any text before
clicking on the WordArt button.

Adding effects to WordArt

You can add some really cool effects to your new WordArt through the WordArt Styles tools.

1 Click your WordArt to open the Drawing Tools toolbar.

2 Click Text Effects.

3 Select the type of effect you want to apply to see a secondary menu.

4 Select the effect to apply it or hover over an effect to see a preview.

 HOT TIP: With the drawing tools open, you can also add shapes to your document.

? DID YOU KNOW?
You can quickly change your WordArt style from the WordArt Drawing Tools toolbar.

Adding Text Effects

Text doesn't have to be WordArt to get some special effects. That's what Text Effects is for!

1 Click the Home tab on the Ribbon.

2 Select some text to add effects to.

3 Click the Text Effects button in the Font Group.

4 Click the type of effect you want to apply.

5 Hover your cursor over the various effects to see a preview in your document.

6 Click the effect you want to apply.

HOT TIP: You can clear all of your text effects by selecting Clear Text Effects from the primary menu.

ALERT: You might have to increase your font size to see some of the effects.

Adding a watermark

People add watermarks to documents that they don't want to be copied. If the document is copied, the watermark is visible and usually identifies the original owner.

1 Click the Page Layout tab from the Ribbon.

2 Click Watermark to expand the menu.

3 Click one of the pre-made watermarks or click Custom Watermark to make your own.

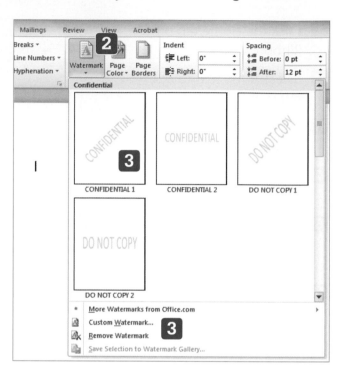

DID YOU KNOW?

You can select Custom to change the visibility of the watermark, making it darker or lighter.

8 Using tables and charts

Introduction

If you deal with any type of data on a regular basis, you'll find using tables and charts to present your information helpful. You can perform many of the basic tasks that you'd normally find in Excel, right here in Word. You'll soon be able to design a table, manipulate cells, design charts and then put it all together at the end.

Inserting a new table

A lot of Word documents begin with tables, in the shape of lists and forms, for example. Designing a blank table is easy in Word 2010. There's two ways you can do it.

1 Click Insert.

2 Click Table.

3 Draw the number of columns and rows that you want in the grid or click Insert Table and enter the information into the dialogue box.

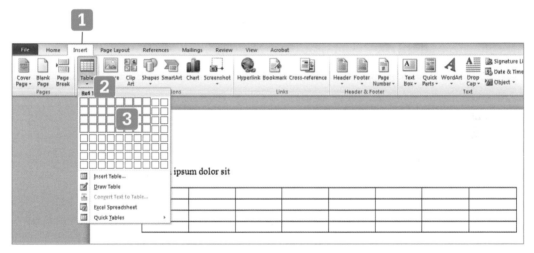

HOT TIP: If you want some creative inspiration or to start out from a template, check out the Quick Tables options from the Table menu.

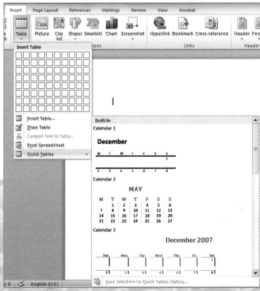

? DID YOU KNOW?

Don't worry if you aren't sure how large your table should be. You'll be able to edit it later.

Drawing a table

There's another way that you can add a new table to your Word document. You can use the Draw Table feature.

1 Click the Insert tab on the Ribbon.

2 Click Table.

3 Click Draw Table.

4 Click-drag your cursor (which now looks like a pencil) to create a table.

5 Let go of the mouse button to finish.

6 Add columns and rows by click-dragging your mouse across the frame of your table.

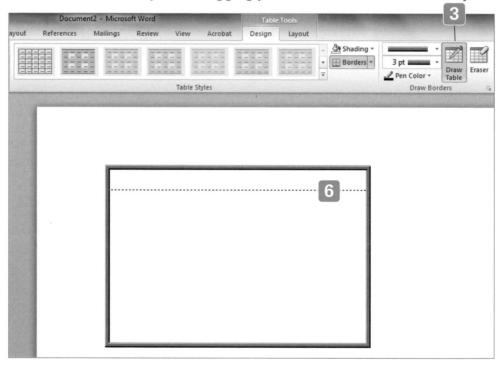

HOT TIP: You can change the colour of your Pen tool by using the drop-down colour menu in the Table Tools toolbar.

? DID YOU KNOW?

Once your table is complete, you can add or delete rows and add Table Styles.

Adding and deleting rows

Once you have the basic shape of your table outlined in your document, you can add or delete rows to accommodate additional data.

1 Click your table to select it and open the Table Tools toolbar.

2 Add rows by using the Draw Table tool or by selecting Insert from the right-click menu.

3 Remove rows by using the Table Eraser or by selecting Delete from the right-click menu.

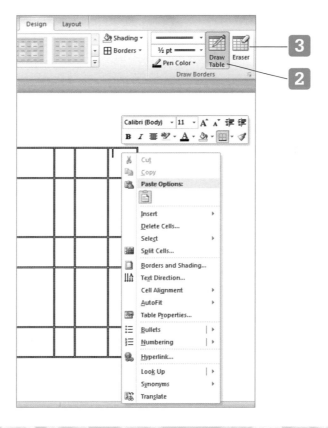

HOT TIP: Click the arrow in the corner of the Draw Borders box to reach the expanded menu.

HOT TIP: If you just want to remove the last row or column that you placed, it's quicker to hit the Undo button instead of erasing or deleting it.

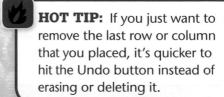

Changing cell height and width

Depending on how much information you want visible in each cell of your table, you may want to widen or narrow cells.

1 Click on your table to select it and open the Table Tools toolbar.

2 Click the Layout tab in the Table Tools toolbar.

3 Enter the size you want for the cells in the Cell Size boxes or use the arrows instead.

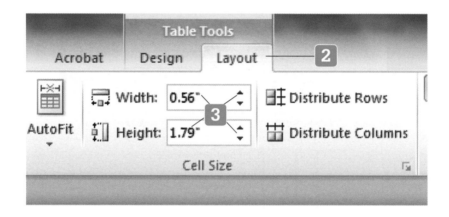

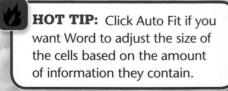 **HOT TIP:** Click Auto Fit if you want Word to adjust the size of the cells based on the amount of information they contain.

 **DID YOU KNOW?**

If you draw a table and the columns aren't even, you can select Distribute Rows or Distribute Columns to even them out.

Formatting cells

You can make other formatting changes to your table cells. You can change the alignment and text wrapping features from the Properties dialogue.

1 Click your table to select it and open the Table Tools toolbar.

2 Click Properties.

3 Change the alignment and text wrapping in the resulting Table Properties dialogue box.

4 Change the alignment of the text within the cells from the Cell tab.

5 Click OK to finish.

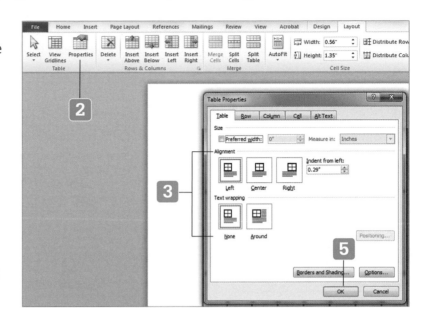

Merging and splitting cells

Sometimes it's necessary to combine cells, for example to create a larger space for a heading. Once you've merged them, you can reverse your actions by splitting the cells back up.

1 Click the table to select it and open the Table Tools toolbar.

2 Select the cells in your table that you want to merge.

3 Click Merge Cells in the Merge group.

4 Click your merged cell and select Split Cells to divide your cells again.

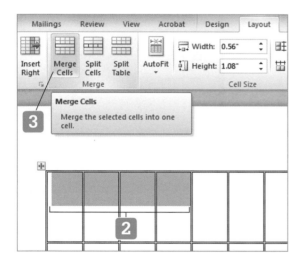

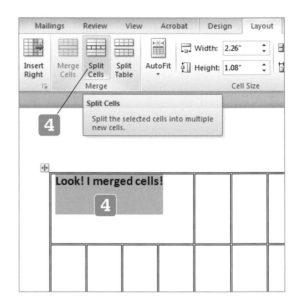

HOT TIP: Merge the top cells together in a table and add some shading for a nice table heading.

? DID YOU KNOW?

You can split tables too. Use Split Table to turn your single table into two separate ones.

Repeat headings

If you are creating a multi-page table with headings, you can choose to have those headings repeated on each page. This helps your readers find information quickly without having to refer to previous pages to find out which column contains what information.

1 Create your table using the Table Tools toolbar.

2 Format your heading row.

3 Click Layout in the Table Tools toolbar tabs.

4 Click Repeat Headings.

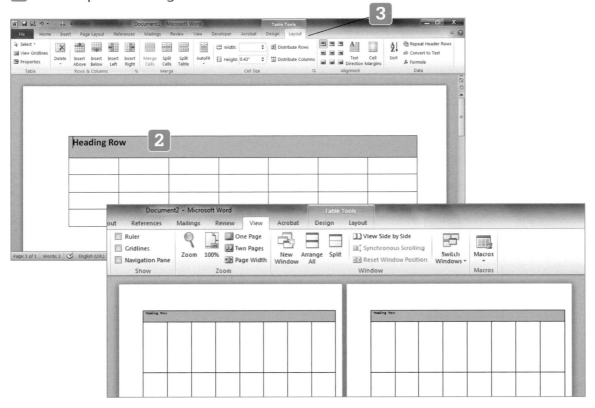

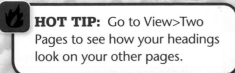

HOT TIP: Go to View>Two Pages to see how your headings look on your other pages.

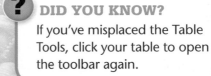

DID YOU KNOW?

If you've misplaced the Table Tools, click your table to open the toolbar again.

Copying and pasting cells

Just like with regular text, you can copy and paste data from one table into another.

1 Click-drag to select text within your table.

2 Copy selected text using either Ctrl-C or the Copy button from the Home tab.

3 Select cells to copy your data into.

4 Paste your information using Ctrl-V or the Paste button from the Home tab.

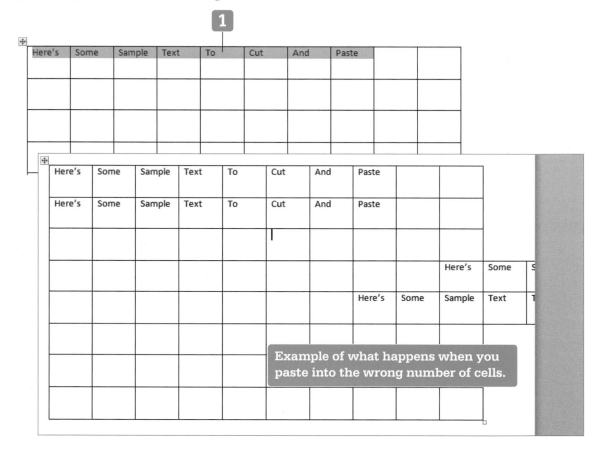

Example of what happens when you paste into the wrong number of cells.

ALERT: You should select the same number of cells to paste to as you did to copy from. Otherwise, when you paste your data, it may alter the destination table's format, as shown here.

HOT TIP: If you need to copy all of the data in a table, use Ctrl-A to select all cells and Ctrl-C to copy them.

Converting a table to text

There's an easy way to get rid of a table while keeping the text. You can convert your table using the Convert to Text feature.

1 Click your table to select it and open the Table Tools.

2 Click Layout in the Table Tools tabs.

3 Click Convert to Text.

4 Select how you want your data separated.

5 Click OK to convert the table.

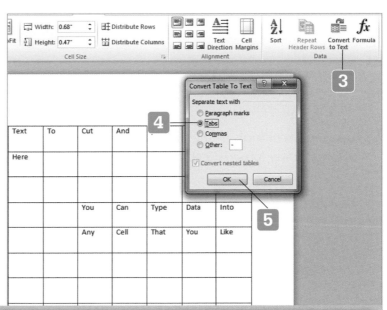

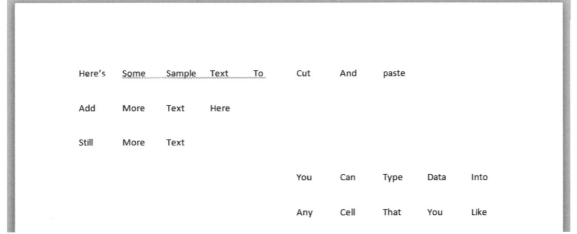

ALERT: Clicking Convert to Text will convert your entire table. If you don't like the new format, click Undo to go back and select another option.

HOT TIP: Experiment with the Separate Text options. One option may work better over another depending on what type of document you are working on.

Inserting Excel spreadsheets

If you need more functionality than you can find in a regular table, you can easily insert an Excel spreadsheet into your document.

1 Click Insert.

2 Click Table.

3 Select Excel Spreadsheet from the drop-down menu.

4 Use the Excel tools in the Ribbon to arrange your spreadsheet.

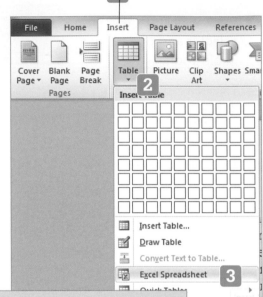

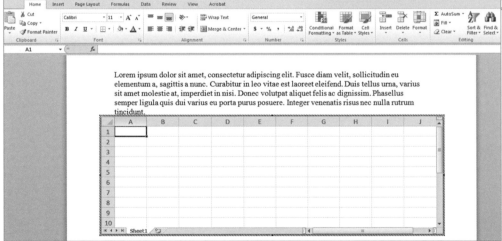

HOT TIP: Once you've inserted an Excel spreadsheet, you can copy and paste from another spreadsheet into the one in your document.

DID YOU KNOW?

If you click the text portion of your document, the Excel spreadsheet closes. Click your spreadsheet to reactivate the tools and edit your data.

Inserting a chart

Word 2010 includes a wide variety of colourful charts for graphically presenting data in your documents.

1 Click the Insert tab on the Ribbon.

2 Click Chart.

3 Click the type of chart you want to add.

4 Click OK to add the chart to your document.

5 Change the data in the resulting Excel spreadsheet to adjust chart values.

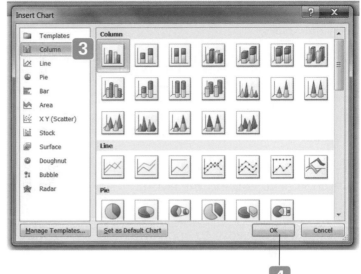

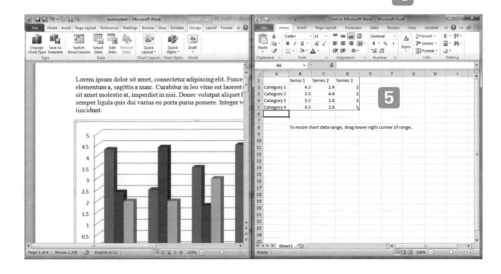

HOT TIP: Click on Edit Data if you want to make further alterations to your chart after you've closed the Excel file.

HOT TIP: Click and select the chart title to edit it.

Applying a new chart layout and style

Once you have your chart created, you can change the layout and style to suit your personal tastes.

1. Click the Chart to select it and open the Chart Tools toolbar.

2. Click Design in the Chart Tools tabs.

3. Click the arrows on the scrollbar to expand the layout menu.

4. Click a new layout to apply it to your chart.

5. Click the arrows on the scrollbar to expand the Chart Styles menu.

6. Click a new style to apply it to your chart.

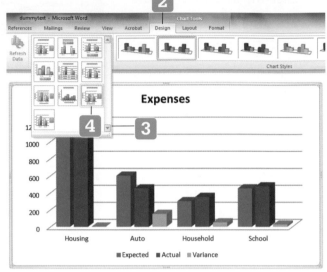

Changing a chart type

Just because you select one type of chart to insert doesn't mean you're wedded to your decision. If you later decide that another chart type would represent your data better, you can always change it.

1 Click the chart to select it and open the Chart Tools toolbar.

2 Click Design in the Chart Tools tabs.

3 Click Change Chart Type.

4 Select a new chart style.

5 Click OK to apply it.

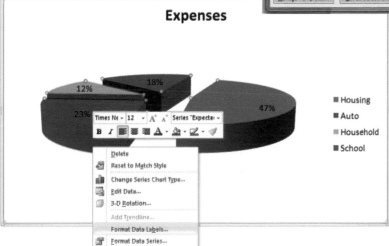

ALERT: You may need to select a new Chart Layout if your new chart type doesn't include the same elements as the old one.

HOT TIP: Right-click on the Chart elements to access an editing menu.

Changing chart labels

When you select a chart, the labels are already in place. You can use the Chart Tools to change which labels appear and where.

1 Click the chart to select it and open the Chart Tools.

2 Click Layout in the Chart Tools tabs.

3 Click the buttons in the Label group to see your options.

4 Click a label option to apply it.

5 Click More Title Options to see the advanced design menu.

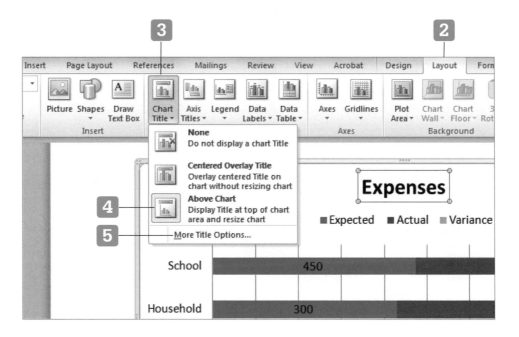

 DID YOU KNOW?
You can change the colour, border and effects of your labels through the advanced menu.

HOT TIP: Use the Labels group to hide labels that don't apply to your chart.

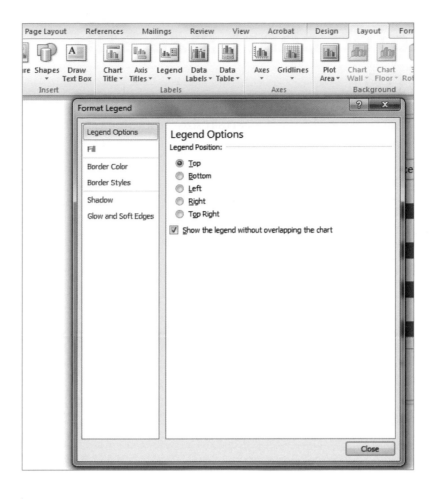

HOT TIP: Select Legends from the Labels menu to show a legend of your applied labels.

Changing chart size and position

Word automatically creates charts of a certain size. You can easily change these settings by using the Chart Tools.

1 Click the chart to open Chart Tools.

2 Click Format in the Chart Tools tabs.

3 Use the arrows or type a new size in the Size group.

4 Click Position to change the position of your chart in relation to the text.

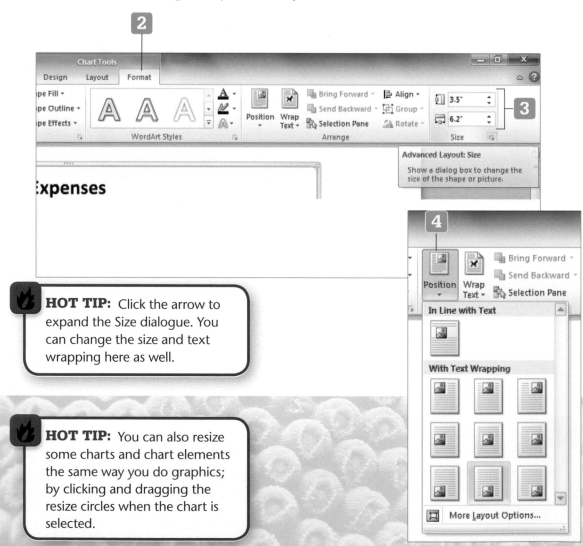

HOT TIP: Click the arrow to expand the Size dialogue. You can change the size and text wrapping here as well.

HOT TIP: You can also resize some charts and chart elements the same way you do graphics; by clicking and dragging the resize circles when the chart is selected.

9 Lists and outlines

Introduction

In all but the most casual writing, organisation is critical. Word provides many ways to organise your information. You can add bulleted or numbered lists, create detailed outlines or design checklists that users can print out or use directly in Word.

Creating a bulleted list

Bullets can emphasise or summarise important information and can help you create lists, meeting agendas and more.

1 Click the Home Tab on the Ribbon.

2 Place your insertion point in your document with your cursor.

3 Click Bullets.

4 Type your first entry after the bullet.

5 Hit enter on your keyboard to move to the next bullet.

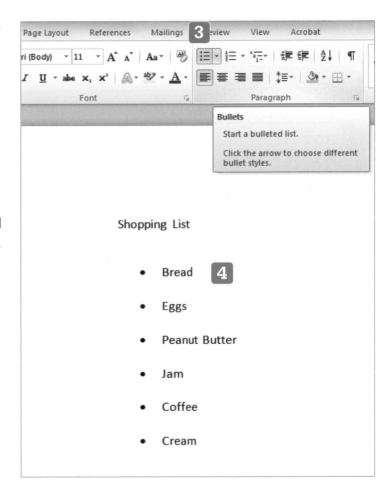

Bullets

Start a bulleted list.

Click the arrow to choose different bullet styles.

Shopping List

- Bread
- Eggs
- Peanut Butter
- Jam
- Coffee
- Cream

 HOT TIP: To stop your bulleted list, you can click the Bullet button again or simply backspace to remove the last bullet from the list.

? DID YOU KNOW?
You should use bullets when there is no hierarchy or specific sequence to your list.

Customising the bullet format

While the standard bullet is a black dot, if you prefer living on the edge, you can change your bullets to a different shape like a star or diamond.

1 Click the Home tab on the Ribbon.

2 Click the arrow in the Bullets button.

3 Select a new bullet style from the menu.

HOT TIP: Use the Live Preview feature to see what the new bullet style will look like in your document.

DID YOU KNOW?

Microsoft has already got you started with some pre-made lists. When you create a new document, check out the templates that are available under the Lists heading.

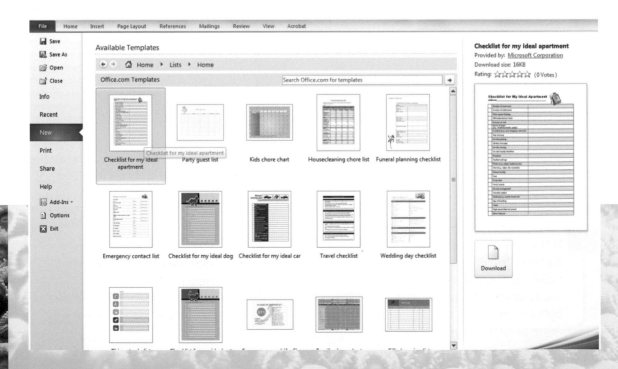

Using pictures or symbols as bullets

You don't have to stick to boring dots and arrows. You can add cool pictures and symbols as your bullet points too.

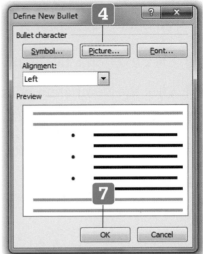

1 Click the Home tab on the Ribbon.

2 Click the arrow on the Bullets button.

3 Click Define New Bullet.

4 Select Picture or Symbol as the bullet type that you want to define.

5 Select an image to use from the resulting menu.

6 Click OK to preview.

7 Click OK again to apply the new bullet style to your list.

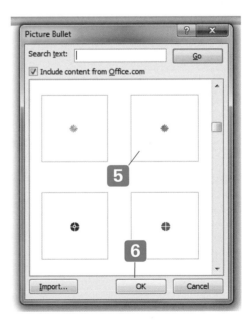

 HOT TIP: Once you've used a bullet style it's added to your gallery. Now that bullet is available from the primary Bullets menu on the Home tab.

? DID YOU KNOW?

You can design and import your own images for bullets. Just remember they need to be very small images. Most bullets are approximately 13 × 13 pixels in size.

Creating a numbered list

When you want to call attention to a specific order in your list, you should use numbers instead of bullets.

1 Click the Home tab on the Ribbon.

2 Click the Numbering button in the Paragraph group.

3 Enter your text after the number 1.

4 Hit enter to continue your list.

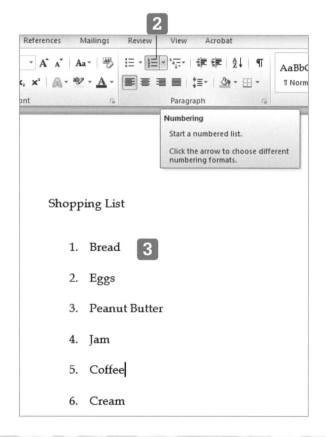

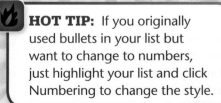

HOT TIP: If you originally used bullets in your list but want to change to numbers, just highlight your list and click Numbering to change the style.

? DID YOU KNOW?

The Numbering Library also includes Roman numerals for outlines and other multi-level lists.

Customising number formats

Just as with the bullets, you can customise your numbering too.

1 Click the Home tab on the Ribbon.

2 Click the arrow on the Numbering button to expand the menu.

3 Select a new numbering style from the list or choose Define New Number Format.

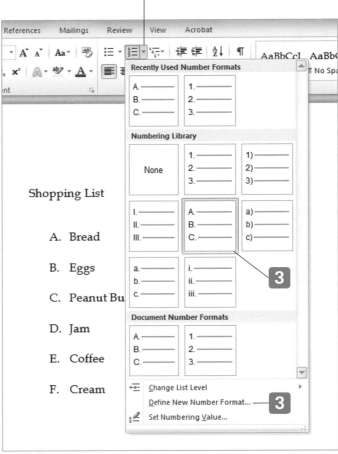

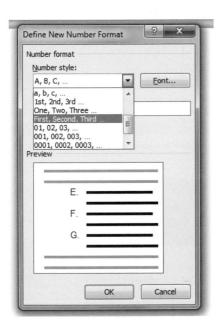

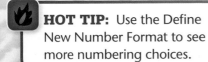

HOT TIP: Use the Define New Number Format to see more numbering choices.

? DID YOU KNOW?

You can change the numbering values of your list so that it starts at any number you choose. While working on an active list, select Set Numbering Value from the Numbering menu.

Continuing a numbered list

Occasionally, you may need to break up a numbered list to insert a graphic or text. You can continue where you left off with automatic numbering.

1 Click the Home tab on the Ribbon.

2 Click Numbering to start your numbered list.

3 Create a few list items.

4 Hit enter to go to the next line and delete the automatic number.

5 Type your text or insert your image.

6 Click Numbering again.

7 Click the lightning bolt that appears and select Continue Numbering.

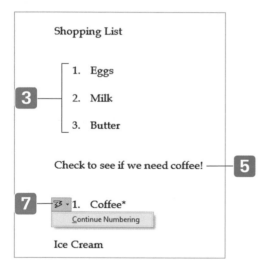

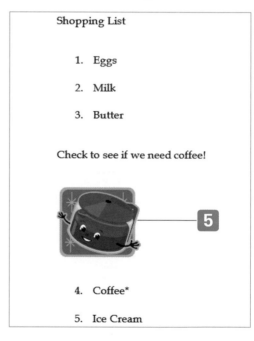

Turning automatic numbering on and off

You don't have to click the Numbering button to start a numbered list. Just start typing 1. And hit enter. Word will automatically start numbering your other list entries. If you don't like this feature, you can turn it off.

1 Click File on the Ribbon.

2 Click Options.

3 Click Proofing.

4 Click AutoCorrect Options.

5 Untick the boxes for Automatic bulleted lists and Automatic numbered lists.

6 Click OK to apply your changes.

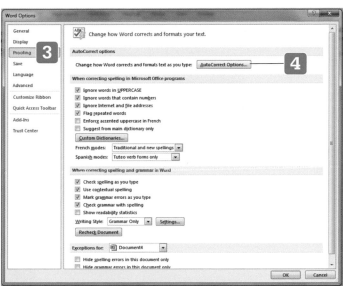

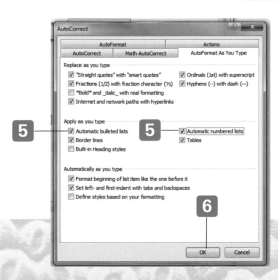

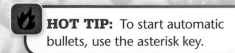

HOT TIP: To start automatic bullets, use the asterisk key.

? DID YOU KNOW?

You can change your automatic numbering settings for your current session only by clicking the lightning bolt when Word first starts auto-numbering.

Combining lists

If you've created two different lists, you can easily combine them into one.

1 Select the text from your second list that you want to add to the first.

2 Drag the text to the line just below the first list.

3 Let go of the mouse button to merge the lists. As shown here the numbers continue consecutively.

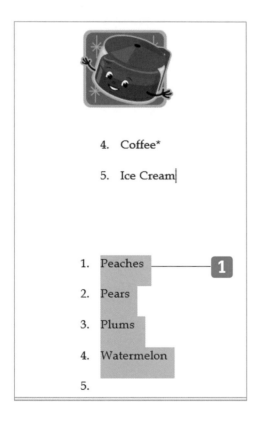

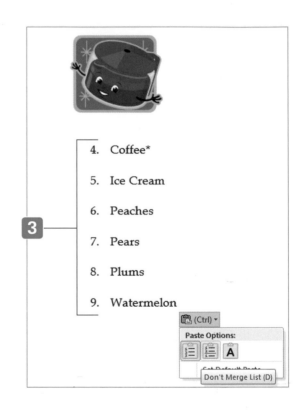

HOT TIP: When you merge your lists, you'll see the Paste Options menu appear on your screen. Click this to see more merging options.

HOT TIP: The Paste Options menu will appear whenever you paste something into your document. You can click on it to see formatting and other options when appropriate.

Alphabetising lists

Once you've created your list, you can easily sort it alphabetically.

1. Click the Home tab on the Ribbon.

2. Select the items or the list that you want to sort.

3. Click Sort.

4. Select how you want your information sorted from the Sort Text dialogue box.

5. Click OK to sort your list.

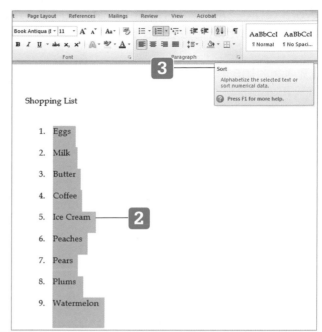

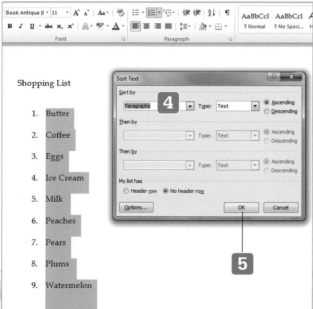

 ALERT: Clicking Sort when there are other elements like images or text blocks within your list will cause formatting issues in your document.

 HOT TIP: Don't want your list sorted after all? Click Undo to go back.

Creating a checklist to print

Word is great for creating checklists. You can design your list in Word and then print out copies when you need them.

1 Click the Insert tab on the Ribbon.

2 Click Insert Table.

3 Create a table with two columns and as many rows as you like.

4 Move your cursor to the top of the uppermost left cell until your cursor becomes an arrow.

5 Click to select the entire column.

6 Click the Home tab.

7 Click Bullets and open the Bullet menu.

8 Click Define Custom Bullet.

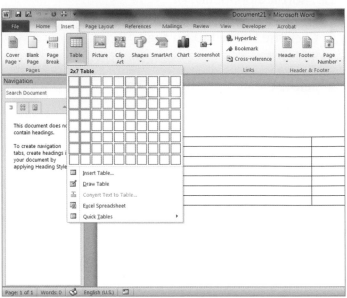

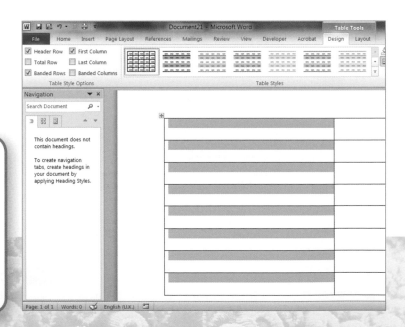

HOT TIP: Since your list is actually a table, you can use the Table Tools to make changes to it: add or delete rows, change the contents alignment or turn on and off the cell borders.

9 Select Symbol and find a box symbol.

10 Click OK to preview.

11 Click OK to apply the boxes to your selected column, as shown here.

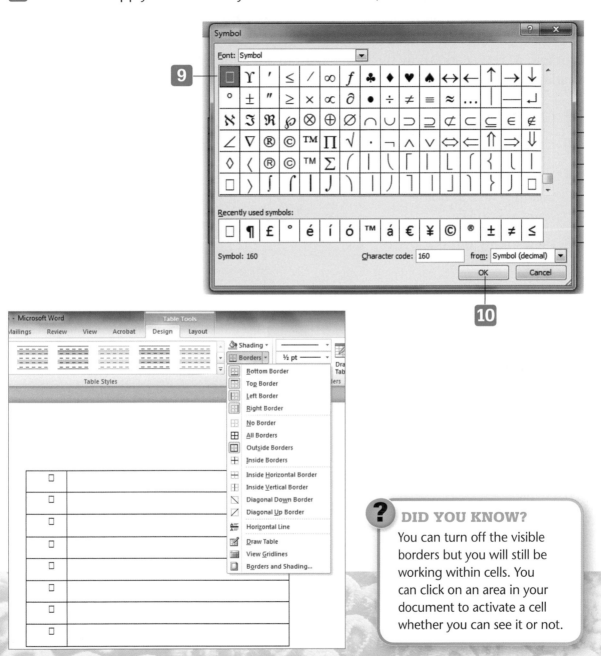

? DID YOU KNOW?

You can turn off the visible borders but you will still be working within cells. You can click on an area in your document to activate a cell whether you can see it or not.

Creating a checklist for use in Word

You can create lists with tickboxes that you or other users can tick off without having to print them out. You'll need to use the Developer tab which is hidden by default. See Problem 5: How can I show the Developer tab, for additional information on how to display it.

1 Click Insert.

2 Click Table.

3 Insert a table with two columns and as many rows as you like.

4 Click OK to add the chart to your document.

5 Click the Developer tab.

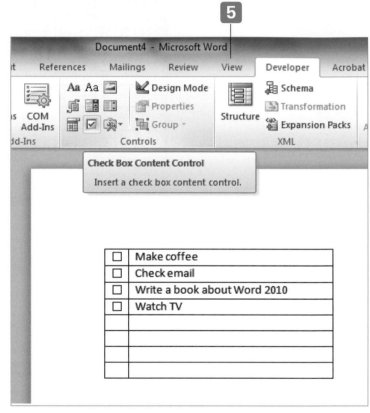

 ALERT: Once you lock the document, you will not be able to edit it unless you turn off the restrictions. Unauthorised users will not be able to turn restrictions on and off.

6 Click in the upper left cell in your table.

7 Click the Checkbox button to add tickboxes down the left side of the table.

8 Adjust the formatting and enter the list text.

9 Lock the document by clicking Developer>Restrict Editing.

10 Click Editing Restrictions and select Filling in Forms.

11 Click Yes, Start Enforcing Restrictions, to lock the form.

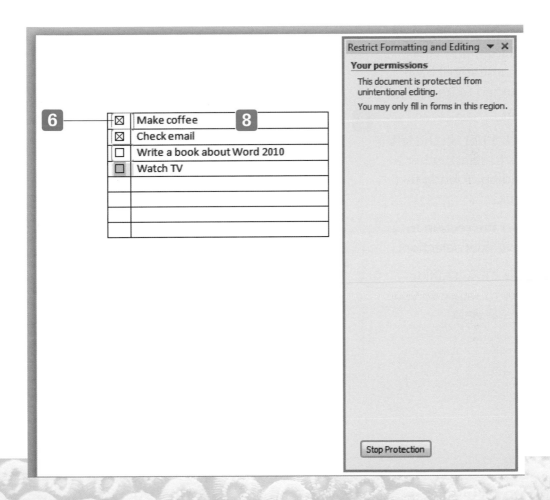

Restrict Formatting and Editing ▼ ✕

Your permissions

This document is protected from unintentional editing.

You may only fill in forms in this region.

6	☒	Make coffee **8**
	☒	Check email
	☐	Write a book about Word 2010
	☐	Watch TV

Stop Protection

HOT TIP: If you want to create forms, you can use the same principles that apply to checklists. Explore the Developer tab for more ideas.

Using the Outline view

If you're an academic, write for a living or happen to be a paragon of organisation, you probably use outlines a lot. Word 2010 has some great features to help you create detailed, professional outlines for your projects.

1 Click View.

2 Click Outline in the Document Views group and a new tab will appear called Outlines, and your document will have changed to an outline form.

3 Click a dot on the left side to select either a heading or body text block.

4 Drag the section to move your selection.

5 Click Close Outline View to return to your normal view.

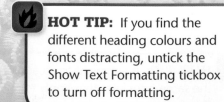

HOT TIP: Click the Show Level drop-down menu to hide all but the specified level.

HOT TIP: If you find the different heading colours and fonts distracting, untick the Show Text Formatting tickbox to turn off formatting.

Promoting headings

When working in outline form, you are assigning a level of importance to each section of your outline. As you work, the importance levels for a heading or section may change. You can easily promote and demote headings using the Outline tools.

1 Click the dot next to the section you want to work with.

2 Click the drop-down menu that currently says Body Text.

3 Select a new level to assign to your selected text.

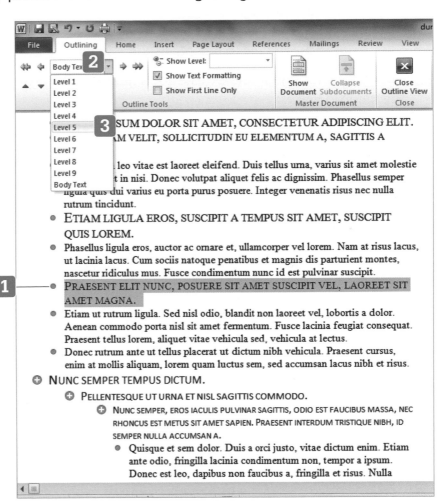

Expanding headings

If you've noticed the little + signs next to some of your outline sections, then you've probably worked out that those are headings with subheadings beneath them. You can hide these subheads to view additional headings and then expand them when you need to see the subheads again.

1 Click a dot in the outline that contains the + symbol.

2 Click the minus sign in the Outline Tools group to shrink the subheads, leaving only the heading visible.

3 Click the plus sign in the Outline Tools group to expand the headings again.

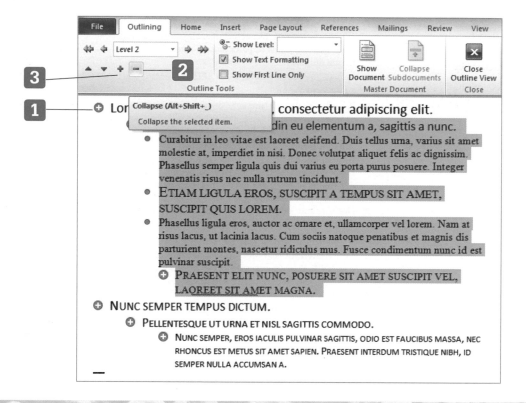

10 Language, research and spelling

Introduction

Not everyone is a natural-born writer but by using Word's language and research tools you'll have access to tools that can help you look like you are. Spell checking will make sure that your document is free from misspelled words and the built-in grammar checker will help identify obvious grammatical errors. When you can't find the perfect words, let Word's thesaurus suggest some ideas. These are just a few of the tools that Word 2010 provides to help you create better, more professional documents.

Checking spelling and grammar automatically

Nothing can hurt a résumé or business report more than typos, misspelled words and poor grammar. Word can help you by checking these areas automatically while you type. You can turn this feature on and off through Word's options.

1 Click the File tab on the Ribbon.

2 Click Options.

3 Click Proofing.

4 Tick the Check spelling as you type box under the When correcting spelling and grammar in Word heading.

5 Tick the Mark grammar errors as you type box.

6 Click OK to apply changes.

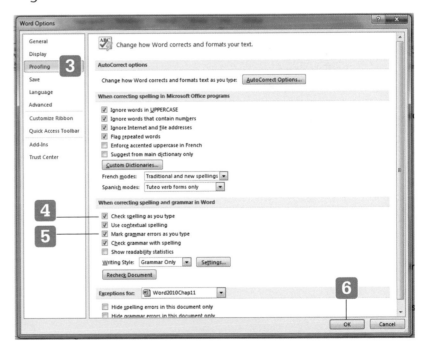

 HOT TIP: If you don't want to see the errors in your document while you work, you can create an exception in the Proofing options dialogue. Just tick the boxes that say Hide Spelling Errors and Hide Grammar Errors in this document only.

? DID YOU KNOW?

Checking spelling and grammar are on by default.

Correcting spelling errors as you type

If automatic spell checking is turned on, Word will mark your spelling errors with a wavy red line. This is your opportunity to correct them.

1 Locate a misspelled word in your document by looking for the wavy red line.

2 Right-click the misspelled word.

3 Select the correct word from the provided suggestions to correct it.

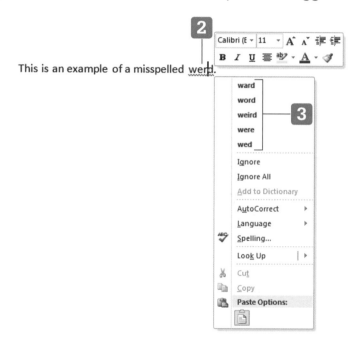

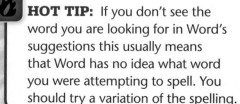

🔥 **HOT TIP:** If you don't see the word you are looking for in Word's suggestions this usually means that Word has no idea what word you were attempting to spell. You should try a variation of the spelling.

❓ **DID YOU KNOW?**
Word will occasionally mark proper names as misspelled. Instead of picking a new word from the provided list, click Add to Dictionary or Ignore All to stop Word from marking the name as incorrect.

Checking spelling manually

Correcting spelling while you type is a personal preference. Some people prefer to write their entire document and then check spelling manually when they are done.

1 Click the Review tab.

2 Click Spelling & Grammar.

3 Click the correct word from the suggestions in the resulting dialogue box.

4 Click Change to correct the word.

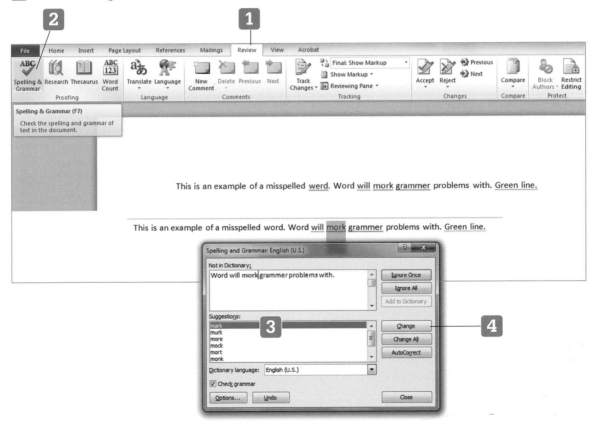

HOT TIP: Word will continue through the errors in your document. In addition to correcting misspelled words, you have the option to ignore a single instance or all instances of a misspelling in your document.

DID YOU KNOW?

If you don't want Word to check your grammar at the same time as spelling, untick the Check grammar box in the Spelling & Grammar window. You can always tick it again for grammar later.

Correcting grammatical errors

Word can also helpfully point out common grammatical errors like sentence fragments and subject-verb agreement.

1 Click the Review tab.

2 Click Spelling & Grammar.

3 Review Word's suggestions and select an appropriate one from the list or correct your sentence as Word suggests.

4 Click Next Sentence to skip to the next grammar error in your document.

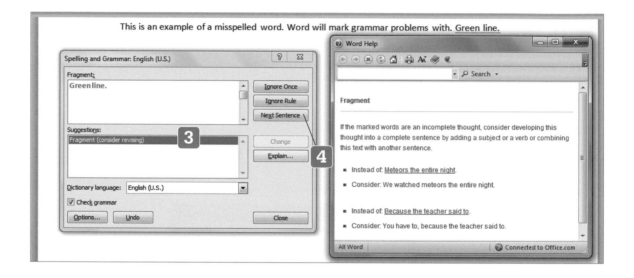

 HOT TIP: Clicking Ignore Rule or correcting the identified error will prompt Word to move to the next issue in your document.

 DID YOU KNOW?
You can click Explain to see the rule that Word is applying to a specific grammar error.

DID YOU KNOW?
You can also right-click on grammar errors and correct them while you type.

Adding words to Spell Check

Try as it might, Word's dictionary isn't perfect. There are some words that it's not familiar with. You can add these words to the custom dictionary.

1 Locate the sentence with the word that you want to add.

2 Right-click the word.

3 Click Add to Dictionary from the options to your right.

4 Click Add to add the word to the dictionary or cancel if not.

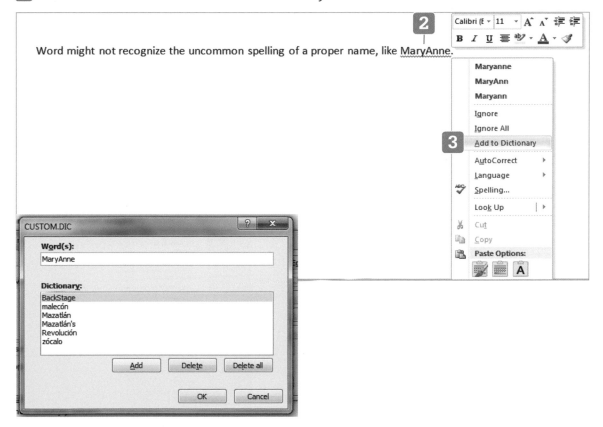

SEE ALSO: Create and use a custom dictionary, in Chapter 2.

DID YOU KNOW?

Once you've added a word to the dictionary, Word won't mark it as misspelled. You must remove it from the custom dictionary if you want it marked as an error in the future.

Using the dictionary

Word's resources can do more than just tell you that a word is misspelled. You also have an entire resource library at your disposal. You can use the dictionary not only to correct misspellings but to look up definitions as well.

1 Right-click the word that you want defined.

2 Select Look Up from the resulting menu.

3 Select Encarta Dictionary.

4 Read the definition that appears in the Research box.

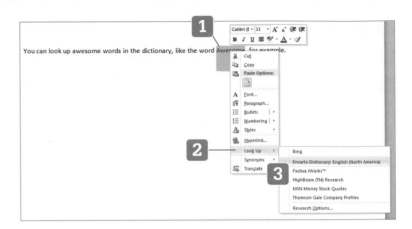

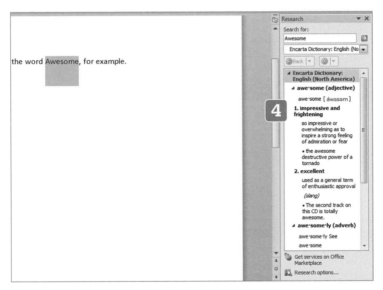

HOT TIP: The dictionary also offers a pronunciation key. Click on the phonetic spelling of the word to see this key and how each of the characters is pronounced.

DID YOU KNOW?

If the word you wanted defined isn't the best fit, use the drop-down menu to select the thesaurus. It will suggest an alternative word to the one you've selected.

Managing research resources

You can select the research resources that are available to you from the Research options. Here you can add other dictionaries to your list, including those in foreign languages.

1 Click the Review tab on the Ribbon.

2 Click Research.

3 Click Research Options at the bottom of the Research window.

4 Click the tickboxes of the resources that you would like to add or untick them to remove them.

5 Click OK to apply your changes.

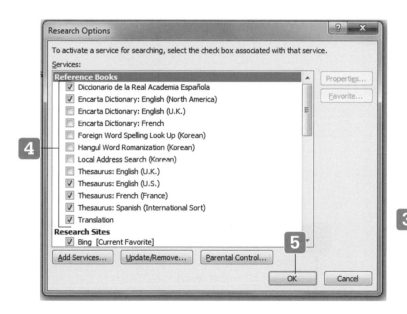

HOT TIP: Once you have your resources added, you can access them through the drop-down menu in the Research window.

DID YOU KNOW?

You can download additional resources for Word from the Office Marketplace. Click Get Services on Office Marketplace from the Research window to see what's available.

Using a foreign language dictionary

Once you've add a foreign language dictionary to your research tools, you can look up words in other languages.

1 Click the Review tab on the Ribbon.

2 Click Research.

3 Type the word you want to search for in the Search bar.

4 Select the appropriate dictionary from the drop-down menu.

5 Click the green arrow to search.

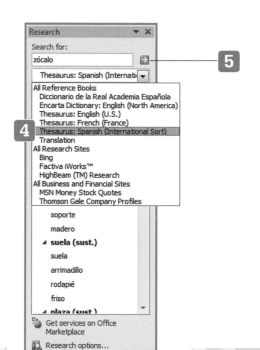

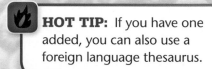

HOT TIP: You can look up a word in the dictionary quickly by pressing ALT and clicking on the word.

HOT TIP: If you have one added, you can also use a foreign language thesaurus.

SEE ALSO: Change the language of Word, in Chapter 2.

Using the thesaurus

The thesaurus tool is invaluable when you can't think of the perfect word to use.

1 Click the Review tab on the Ribbon.

2 Click Thesaurus.

3 Type the word you want synonyms for in the search bar.

4 Select Thesaurus from the drop-down menu if it isn't already selected.

5 Click the green arrow to search.

6 Click a word from the list provided to see more synonyms.

7 Click the arrow that appears by a word to insert it into your text, copy it to the clipboard or look it up in the dictionary.

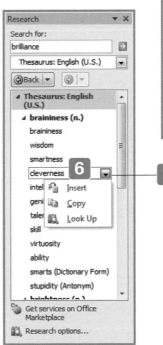

Using Bing to view web search results

You can search the Internet and view a results summary from Word.

1 Click the Review tab on the Ribbon.

2 Click Research.

3 Type the entry that you'd like to search for in the search bar.

4 Select Bing from the drop-down menu.

5 Click the green arrow to search.

6 View the results of your web search in the lower pane.

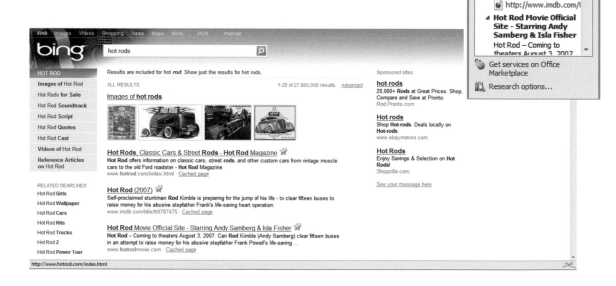

HOT TIP: If you want to see all of the results in your browser, click View All Results on Live Search. Your browser will open and take you to the results on the Bing search page.

DID YOU KNOW?
Clicking the link below the search result will open your browser and take you to that page.

Using Factiva iWorks for research

Factiva iWorks is a business information service that is available through Word 2010. You can quickly research for relevant articles in a variety of publications.

1 Click the Review tab on the Ribbon.

2 Click Research.

3 Type the search phrase into the search bar.

4 Select Factiva iWorks from the drop-down menu.

5 Click the green arrow to search.

6 View results in the lower pane.

 ALERT: You need a registered account to use Factiva iWorks and there is a charge for downloading articles.

 HOT TIP: Use Factiva iWorks to find relevant articles and then check that publication's website. You might find that it offers free access to its archives.

 DID YOU KNOW? Word offers a variety of research tools. Take some time and see what each one has to offer.

Translating text

While it isn't exactly a substitution for having a professional translator on hand, Word can help you by translating basic text into other languages.

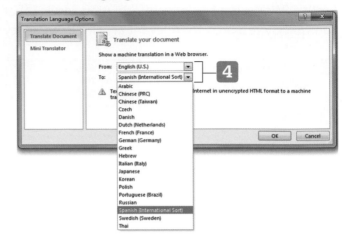

1 Click the Review tab on the Ribbon.

2 Click Translate.

3 Click Translation Language Options.

4 Select a To and From translation language from the drop-down menu.

5 Select some text to translate.

6 Click Translate and select a translation option.

7 View the results in the subsequent Research window.

ALERT: Online translators can be helpful but aren't a substitute for a native language translator. Often, at best, the translated text will be awkward. At worst, it might have an entirely different meaning than you intended! When possible, have a native speaker review your document when using automatic translators.

Finding a word count

There are times when you need to create a document that meets a specific word or character count, for example for a journal article. With Word, you can quickly get the statistics on your document.

1 Click Review.

2 Click Word Count. The statistics will be displayed as shown here.

3 Click Close to close the Word Count box.

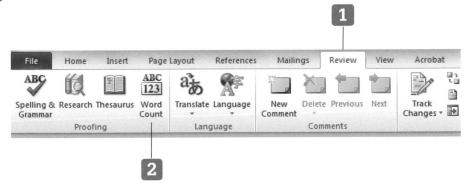

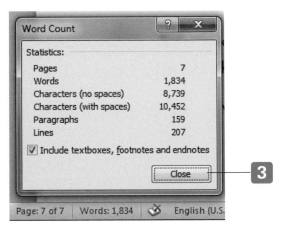

11 Collaboration and co-authoring

Introduction

Tracking changes and adding comments are two of the ways that Word users could collaborate on a document in the past. Now Word 2010, as well as several other Office programs like Excel and PowerPoint, has a feature that allows multiple parties to make changes to shared documents and online workspaces. These advanced collaboration tools allow people to work together on projects even when, geographically, they are far apart.

Tracking changes

Track Changes is a helpful function for keeping track of how you or someone else has edited a document. When Track Changes is on, any changes to the text or formatting will be shown in a different colour, with the author's name and the date of the change.

1 Click Review.

2 Click Track Changes.

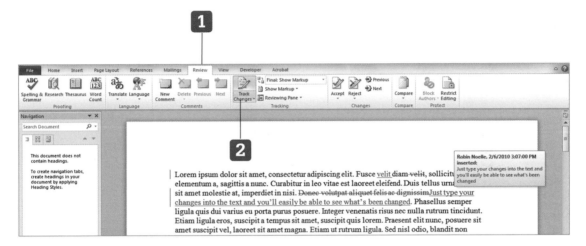

HOT TIP: If you want to turn off Track Changes, just click the button again.

? DID YOU KNOW?
You can fully customise how Word tracks changes. Click the Track Changes button to access the additional menu and select Change Tracking Options. You can set the colour and style of tracked changes from here.

HOT TIP: You can also right-click on a tracked change to turn Track Changes off from the resulting menu options.

Accepting and rejecting tracked changes

Once you've received a document back with someone's proposed changes, it's up to you whether you want to accept those changes or not.

1 Open the document that contains tracked changes.

2 Click Review.

3 Click Next to go to the first tracked change.

4 Click Accept or Reject to incorporate or delete the change and move to the next change.

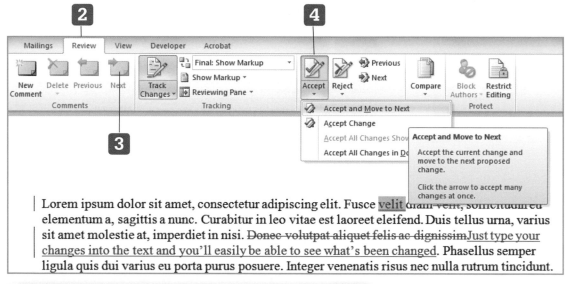

 HOT TIP: You can click the arrow below Accept or Reject to see more options like Accept/Reject All Changes in document.

? DID YOU KNOW?

The default when you click Accept or Reject is to perform the action and then move to the next change, so you don't need to select that from the drop-down menu.

 HOT TIP: Use the Previous and Next buttons to move through all of the changes in your document without accepting or rejecting them.

Showing and hiding markup

Suppose you have a document that's been edited, perhaps by several people. All of that coloured text and those symbols can be confusing if you're just trying to see what one editor suggested. You can control what elements you see in the Markup view and from which authors, all from the Review tab.

1 Click Review.

2 Click the Show Markup arrow to expand the menu.

3 Click the items that you want to appear so that they have a tickmark beside them.

4 Remove the tickmarks from the items you do not want shown.

5 Click Reviewers to select whose changes you want to show.

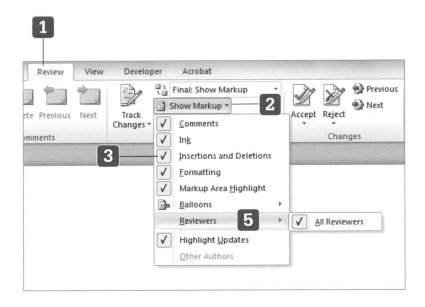

HOT TIP: Use the Show Markup options to select which items you want to display when you print your document. For example, you could choose to print your document showing only comments and insertions from a single author, all changes from all authors or any combination you prefer.

HOT TIP: Do you want a detailed summary of all of the changes in your document? Click Reviewing Pane and a new window will appear with all of the revision information right there.

Changing the Markup view

When you want to refer to the original document prior to tracking changes or to see how the final document will look with your changes incorporated, you can change the Markup view via the Review tab.

- Original/Final: Show Markup – this shows your document with the proposed changes tracked in Markup.

- Original: this shows your document prior to any changes.

- Final: this shows your document with all of the proposed changes incorporated.

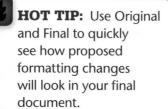 **HOT TIP:** Use Original and Final to quickly see how proposed formatting changes will look in your final document.

HOT TIP: Unless you have several versions of a edited document, you won't see much difference between Final: Show Markup and Original: Show Markup. Later, you can use these to see the first suggested changes and compare them to the proposed changes in the current version.

Printing tracked changes

In a world of computers, smart phones and texting, some people still prefer to do their editing on actual paper documents. To that end, you can print out your document with the tracked changes to see what's been proposed.

1 Open the document that you want to print.

2 Use the Show Markup options to select the elements that you want to appear in your printed document.

3 Click File.

4 Click Print.

5 Click Print All Pages, under Settings, to access the drop-down menu.

6 Click Print Markup if it doesn't already have a tickmark.

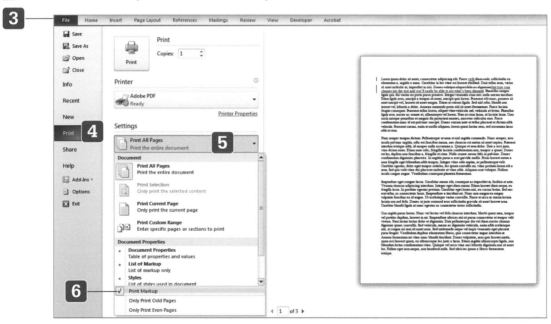

HOT TIP: If you prefer, you can print just a summary of the tracked changes by clicking List of Markup in the above Print options.

HOT TIP: Print your tracked changes on a colour printer to make them easier to see.

Adding and deleting comments

Occasionally when editing or creating documents, you may have a question or comment that isn't a direct change to the text. You can use the New Comment feature to add notes to your document.

1 Click Review.

2 Select text to attach your comment to or place your cursor where you want to add a comment.

3 Click New Comment.

4 Type your comment in the coloured balloon that appears.

5 Click outside of the balloon to keep your comment and get back to your document.

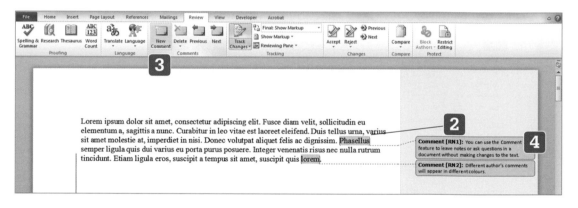

 HOT TIP: Use the Delete Comment action when Accepting or Rejecting Changes to delete comments. You can also right-click on a comment and select Delete from the side menu.

? DID YOU KNOW?
You can use the Change Tracking Options to format the balloons.

HOT TIP: You can use the Show Markup options to select what types of changes appear in balloons; all changes or just comments.

Changing the author's name

As you've probably noticed by now, the name of the person who installed Word is the default author for comments and changes. You can change the author's name so that it accurately reflects the current author.

1 Click Review.

2 Click the Track Changes arrow.

3 Click Change User Name.

4 Type your User Name and Initials in the text boxes.

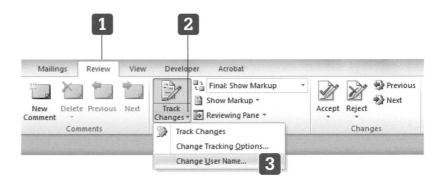

5 Click OK to save your changes and return to your document.

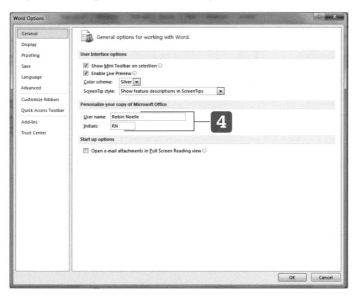

Comparing documents

Comparing documents is useful when you want to see what changes have been made between versions.

1 Click Review on the Ribbon.

2 Click Compare.

3 Click Compare again.

4 Select the first document using the drop-down menu or by browsing.

5 Select a second version to compare it to.

6 Click OK to see the comparison.

ALERT: You should only compare documents that have no tracked changes, otherwise Word assumes they are to be accepted.

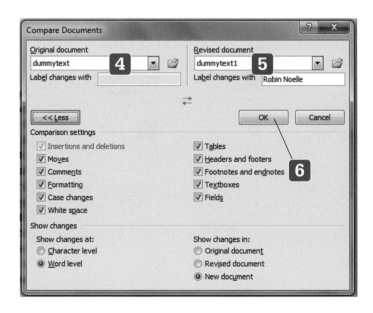

Compare Documents

Original document
dummytext **4**

Label changes with

Revised document
dummytext1 **5**

Label changes with   Robin Noelle

<< Less   **OK**   **Cancel**

6

Comparison settings

☑ Insertions and deletions   ☑ Tables
☑ Moves   ☑ Headers and footers
☑ Comments   ☑ Footnotes and endnotes
☑ Formatting   ☑ Textboxes
☑ Case changes   ☑ Fields
☑ White space

Show changes

Show changes at: Show changes in:
○ Character level   ○ Original document
● Word level   ○ Revised document
                                 ● New document

? DID YOU KNOW?

Comparing documents will show you three versions: the original, the revised and, finally, the two combined with all of the changes highlighted and summarised.

HOT TIP: In the Compare dialogue box, select More to see all of your options.

Combining documents

When you want to see all of the proposed changes from multiple authors, you can simply combine all of the versions of a document into one. Once you do, you'll be able to see all of the changes in one place but still determine who changed what.

1 Click Review on the Ribbon.

2 Click Compare.

3 Click Combine.

4 Select the first document using the drop-down menu or by browsing.

5 Select a second version to combine it with.

6 Click OK to see the two documents combined, as here.

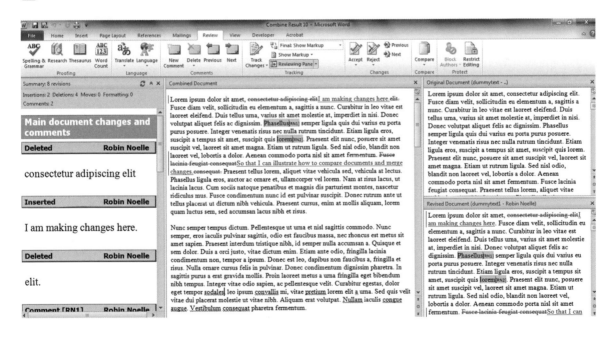

 HOT TIP: If you need more space in your windows, click Reviewing Pane to show it or hide it from view.

 DID YOU KNOW?

Once you've combined two documents, you can combine the result with yet another document to include another author.

Restricting document changes

If you frequently collaborate with people on documents, it's a good idea to restrict changes when you've finally reached a finished product. This lets your co-workers know that no additional changes are being made and prevents accidental editing of completed projects.

1 Click the Review tab on the Ribbon.

2 Click Restrict Editing.

3 Click Editing restrictions: Allow only this type of editing in the document, to activate the drop-down menu.

4 Select the type of restriction to apply.

5 Add exceptions when applicable in the Exceptions box.

6 Click Yes, Start Enforcing Protection to activate the restriction.

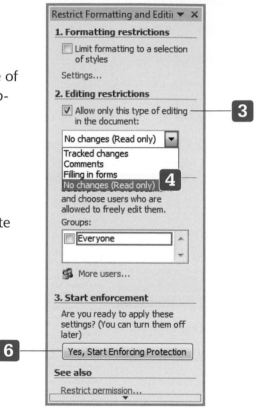

HOT TIP: If you want to prevent changes being made to your document's format, you can set restrictions on formatting as well.

DID YOU KNOW?

You can also restrict formatting to only a few select styles that you choose.

Using Information Rights Management

You can use the free Information Rights Management tools to restrict who can and cannot open, view and edit your documents. While the service is free, you do need a Windows Live ID to use it.

1. Click Review on the Ribbon.

2. Click Restrict Editing.

3. Click Restrict permission to this document.

4. Select that you would like to activate the Information Rights Management Services.

5. Enter your Windows Live ID to activate the service.

6. Click Restrict permission to this document to activate the dialogue box.

7. Enter the email addresses of the people you want to authorise in the appropriate permissions field.

8. Click OK to apply your changes.

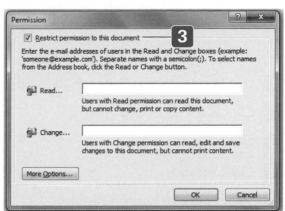

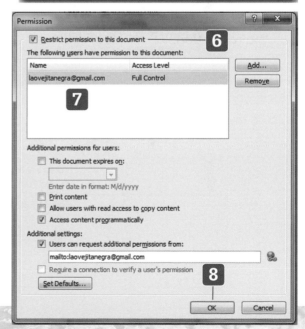

? DID YOU KNOW?

You can click More Options and set a date for your document to expire. After this date, users will not be able to access it.

🔥 HOT TIP: Use Permissions to restrict users from copying sensitive information from your document.

Keeping track of changes with Version Information

One of the great things about sharing documents online is that you don't have to wait for the other person to send your document back to you to see their changes or make more changes of your own. Of course, if you have multiple authors and editors working on a single document, you need to be able to see what the most recent version is. That's where Version Information comes in.

1 Log into Windows Live and go to Office Live Workspaces.

2 Click a document to open it.

3 Make changes.

4 Click Version.

5 Select Save to Version History.

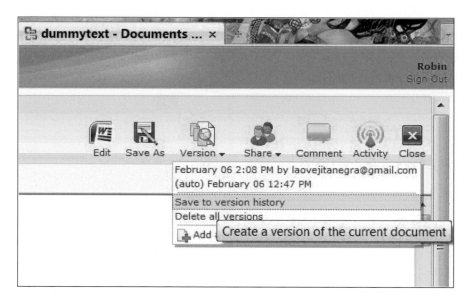

 DID YOU KNOW?

If you've made changes to your document on your computer, select Add a New Document Version to upload it and add it to the version history.

HOT TIP: You can see all of the versions that are available by clicking on Version. The most recent one will be at the top.

12 Online collaboration and Office Live

Introduction

Mobile computing has increased tremendously with the proliferation of free Internet hot spots and affordable laptop models. Now people can work from anywhere; coffee shops, libraries, airports and even while flying! Microsoft Office has addressed the productivity needs of these mobile workers with ways to access Office (and Word) 2010 while on the go.

Getting a Windows Live account

In order to use Office Mobile online, you'll need to sign up for a free Windows Live account. This will give you access to a host of online services that you can use from Microsoft.

1 Visit http://home.live.com.

2 Click Sign Up.

3 Complete the web form.

4 Click I Accept to accept the terms of service.

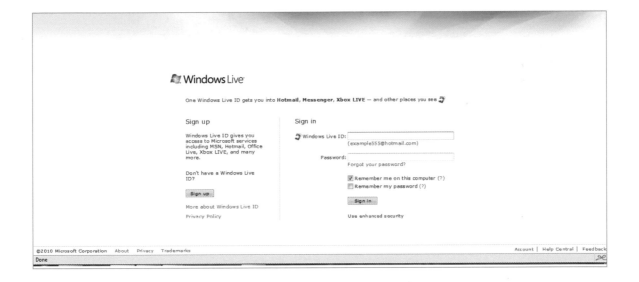

HOT TIP: By signing up for Windows Live, you agree that Microsoft can send you email. Once your account is active, sign in, click on your name and select View Your Account. You can then select Marketing Preferences and unsubscribe if you wish.

? DID YOU KNOW?

If you have a Hotmail, MSN Messenger or xBoxLive account, you already have a Windows Live ID.

Accessing Office Live

Once you have a Windows Live ID, you can sign in and starting exploring what's available to you. Office Live is a free service that allows you to access your documents online and use web versions of Office programs, like Word 2010.

1 Open your browser and visit the Windows Live website.

2 Log in with your Windows Live ID.

3 Click More from the navigation bar at the top of the page.

4 Select Office Live.

5 Click Get Started Here.

6 Click I Accept to accept the terms of service.

7 Click OK.

8 Wait for Office Live to create your account.

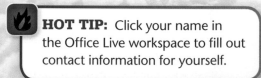

HOT TIP: Click your name in the Office Live workspace to fill out contact information for yourself.

DID YOU KNOW?

Office Live isn't the only online workspace that you can use but it's the only one that offers Microsoft Office programs.

Adding documents to Office Live

Before you can start sharing and editing documents online, you need to upload them to Office Live.

1 Log in to Windows Live and go to the Office Live Workspace page.

2 Click Add Documents.

3 Browse to the location of the document you want to upload.

4 Select the document and click Open.

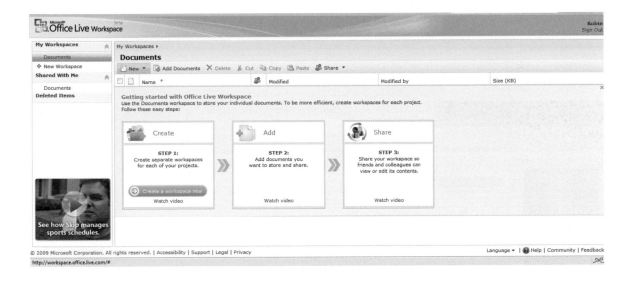

 HOT TIP: You can create individual Workspaces for different projects or document types. You could have a workspace for household management documents like family schedules and budgets and one for work documents, for example.

 ALERT: If you get an upload error, it could be because your document is open in Word on your computer. Close Word and try uploading the document again.

Creating a new document

You can create new documents in Office Live too. Available document types include Word, Excel, Powerpoint and a variety of lists.

1 Log into your Office Live account.

2 Click New.

3 Select Word document from the menu.

4 Wait while Word creates your new document and opens Word.

 ALERT: Depending on your web browser and security settings, you may receive a security warning before Office Live creates your document. It's safe to use Office Live, so go ahead and ignore it.

 DID YOU KNOW?

Word may open your new document in Protected View because it originated on the Internet. Since you created it yourself, go ahead and click Enable Editing.

Saving documents to SkyDrive

You can create documents in Word and then share them online with Microsoft's free SkyDrive service without ever having to open your web browser.

1 Open a document or create a new document to share.

2 Click File.

3 Click Share.

4 Click Save to SkyDrive.

5 Click Sign In to sign in with your Windows Live ID.

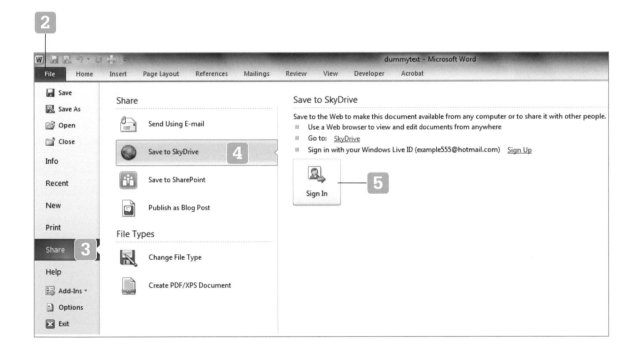

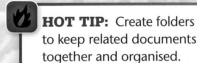 **HOT TIP:** Create folders to keep related documents together and organised.

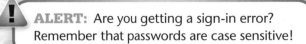 **ALERT:** Are you getting a sign-in error? Remember that passwords are case sensitive!

6 Click Save As.

7 Name your document and click Save.

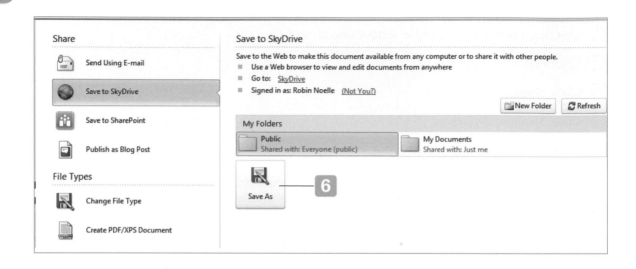

WHAT DOES THIS MEAN?

SkyDrive is a place to store your work online. You upload documents to Microsoft's SkyDrive server and then you can access them from wherever you have Internet access.

Viewing documents in SkyDrive

Once you've uploaded your documents to SkyDrive, you can log in to view, edit or share them from your favourite web browser anywhere.

1 Open your browser and log into Windows Live.

2 Click More on the navigation bar.

3 Click SkyDrive.

4 Click the folder that you saved your document to (Public, most likely).

5 Click the document that you want to view.

6 Click View.

 HOT TIP: Click Open in Word if you want to download and open the document from your computer.

 ALERT: You may have to accept another licensing agreement before you can view your SkyDrive documents in the Office Live Word application.

Sharing documents in SkyDrive

When you upload or share documents to SkyDrive either online or from Word, you have two main options; you can upload them to the public folder giving everyone access or to a private folder that only you can access. You can set other permissions once you've uploaded the file.

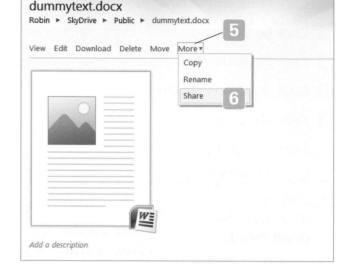

1 Log into your Windows Live account.

2 Click SkyDrive from the More menu in the navigation bar.

3 Click the folder you saved your document to.

4 Click the document you want to share.

5 Click More from the document options.

6 Click Share.

7 Select from the sharing options to invite others to view your document.

 HOT TIP: If you've imported or created a contacts list in Windows Live, you can add your contacts to your invitation email easily with just a click of the mouse button.

? DID YOU KNOW?
You can use the provided HTML to add an icon that leads to your document from a blog or social networking site.

Creating SkyDrive folders to share

You can create special folders for your documents that are shared with only the people you specify. Once you upload your documents into a folder with set permissions, only the people allowed to view that folder will have access to it.

1 Log into Windows Live and access the SkyDrive.

2 Click Create a Folder.

3 Enter a name for your folder.

4 Select Select people from the Share with drop-down menu.

5 Select or add people to share your folder with.

6 Select their permissions level from the drop-down menu.

7 Click Next and add the files you want to share.

8 Click Upload to upload your documents and finish.

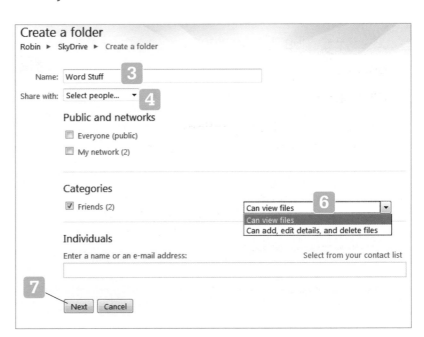

? DID YOU KNOW?
You can determine whether your invitees have permission to simply view your documents or to edit them.

 HOT TIP: Entering the email address of someone you wish to share your document with will send an email to them with a link to your SkyDrive folder.

Sharing Office Live documents

Uploading and sharing documents in the SkyDrive will open the Office Live version of Word, or you can upload your documents right to Office Live Workspaces and share them from there.

1 Log into Windows Live and go to Office Live Workspaces.

2 Click Add Documents to upload a document to share.

3 Click the tickbox next to your document.

4 Click Share.

5 Enter the email addresses of the people you want to invite in the appropriate permissions field.

6 Enter a personal message to explain why you are sharing the document.

7 Click Send.

HOT TIP: Once you've sent your invitation, the authorised users will appear above the document. You can add more users or remove the ones you added from this screen.

DID YOU KNOW?

If you don't click Let everyone view this without signing in, they will need an active Windows Live ID to be able to view your document.

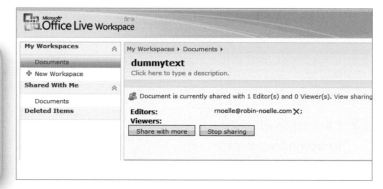

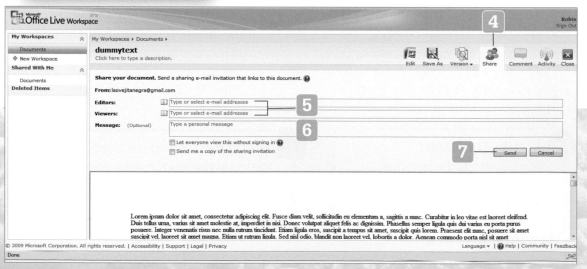

Showing document activity

You'll be able to see who has edited a document and what the most recent version is from the Versions information but if you want more detailed information, you will need to view the activity log.

1 Log into Windows Live and go to Office Live Workspaces.

2 Click a document to open it.

3 Click Activity.

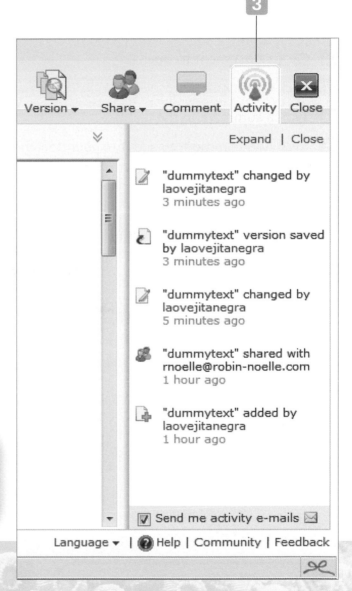

3

Version ▾   Share ▾   Comment   Activity   Close

≫   Expand | Close

📝 "dummytext" changed by laovejitanegra
3 minutes ago

↩ "dummytext" version saved by laovejitanegra
3 minutes ago

📝 "dummytext" changed by laovejitanegra
5 minutes ago

👥 "dummytext" shared with rnoelle@robin-noelle.com
1 hour ago

➕ "dummytext" added by laovejitanegra
1 hour ago

☑ Send me activity e-mails ✉

Language ▾ | ❓ Help | Community | Feedback

HOT TIP: Click Expand to see the document's activity in a larger window.

HOT TIP: Tick the send me activity e-mails to get email updates whenever someone changes your document.

Adding document comments

You can leave messages for your co-collaborators in your shared document. Use the Comments feature to ask questions, leave instructions, make comments or just leave an encouraging word.

1 Log into Windows Live and go to Office Live Workspaces.

2 Click a document to open it.

3 Click Comment.

4 Type a comment in the text box.

5 Click Add comment to add it to your document and make it visible to everyone.

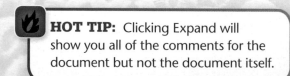
HOT TIP: Clicking Expand will show you all of the comments for the document but not the document itself.

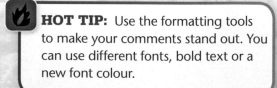
HOT TIP: Use the formatting tools to make your comments stand out. You can use different fonts, bold text or a new font colour.

13 Creating blogs and using web elements

Introduction

If you are like most people, you probably spend at least a portion of your day online; reading email, visiting social networking sites or using the Internet for research. Word can help you put some of your own content online too. Word 2010 supports several popular blog platforms, allowing you to design your blog posts in Word and then upload them quickly and easily. You can also create Word documents that include hyperlinks so that your readers can simply click on a link and be taken to the website that you've referenced. If you want, you can even save your Word documents as HTML and load them onto a server to display as a very basic webpage.

Creating a blog account

The first step to blogging with Word 2010 is to create an account with a blog provider so that you have somewhere to publish your posts. You can create an account at any one of the blog service providers that Office supports, including popular hosts like Blogger, Typepad, WordPress and Windows Live Spaces.

1 Visit the website of your preferred blog host.

2 Click New Account or Sign Up.

3 Complete the web form.

4 Check your email for a confirmation of your account and follow the included instructions to activate your new blog.

5 Write down your username, password and blog URL somewhere where you can easily access them.

 HOT TIP: Check the Microsoft Office Marketplace under Blog Providers for the most current list of supported blog hosts.

? DID YOU KNOW?
Different blog hosts will have different sign-up requirements and procedures. They also offer different features. Take a look at several before selecting the one that's right for you.

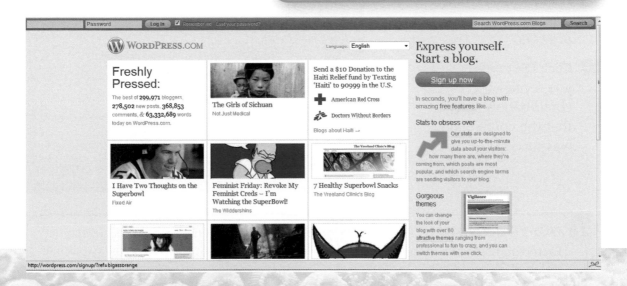

WHAT DOES THIS MEAN?

Blog: this is short for web log. You can find literally thousands of different types of blogs. Some people create photo blogs, blogs for their families, business blogs, sports blogs, music blogs and more!

Registering a blog account

Now that you have a blog account, you need to tell Word what it is so that it knows where to upload your posts. You will need information provided by your blog host when you signed up for your account, so make sure you have that to hand.

1 Click File on the Ribbon.

2 Click New.

3 Click Blog Post.

4 Click Register Now in the Register a Blog Account box.

5 Select your blog provider from the drop-down menu and click Next.

6 Fill in the requested information regarding your blog account.

7 Click OK.

8 Wait for Word to connect to your blog provider.

9 Click OK when you receive the confirmation notice that the connection was successful.

DID YOU KNOW?

Each blog host has a different set up. If you need help filling in the information for your specific provider, click Help me fill out this section and Word will take you to the help file for your blog provider's services.

HOT TIP: There's no reason to change the Picture Options unless you plan on using a picture host that is different from your blog provider.

HOT TIP: You can add multiple blog accounts to Word. Just use the Manage Accounts button in the Blog post tab to add, remove or change account information.

Creating a blog post

Creating a new blog post in Word is as easy as creating a new document.

1 Click File.

2 Click New.

3 Click Blog Post.

4 Click Create.

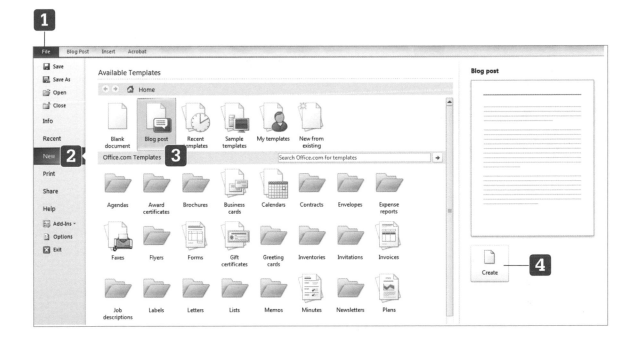

 HOT TIP: You can choose to add the Blog post tab to the Ribbon through the File>Options>Customise the Ribbon options.

? DID YOU KNOW?

When you are creating a blog post, only the tabs and features of Word that are compatible for blog formatting and posting will be available.

Uploading a blog post

Once you've created a blog post, it's time to put it online for the visitors to your blog to view. You can do this with the Publish button.

1 Create a new blog post.

2 Write your post and enter a title.

3 Click Publish to send your post to your blog host.

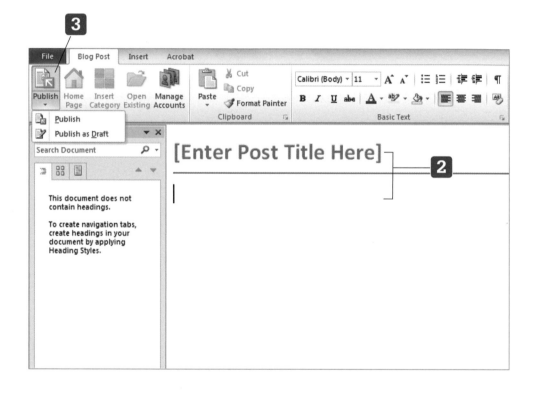

 HOT TIP: You can upload your post as a draft and then make changes online from your blog account dashboard before finalising and making it live.

4 Wait while Word connects with your blog. A confirmation will appear in your document.

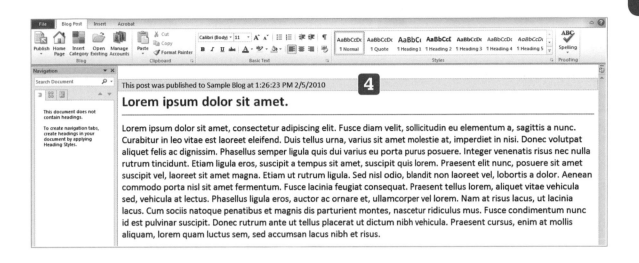

 **DID YOU KNOW?**

If you are having trouble posting to your blog, double-check that your user name and password are correct and that your post has a title.

Editing an existing blog post

You can visit your blog's dashboard and edit your existing posts or you can easily open them in Word, make changes and upload the new version.

1 Click Blog Post.

2 Click Open Existing.

3 Select the blog post you want to open.

4 Click OK.

5 Edit your post.

6 Click Publish to update your blog with the new version.

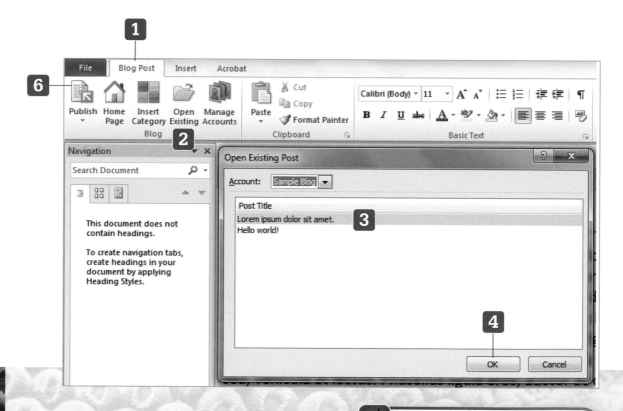

ALERT: If you don't see your updated post when you visit your blog, click Refresh in your browser to make sure it is showing the most current version.

HOT TIP: Word will update your document every time you post it so you always know the last date you made changes and uploaded it to your site.

Adding a category to your blog post

Categories don't just help readers find the information that's important to them, it also helps search engines to find and categorise your blog.

1 Open a blog post or create a new one.

2 Click Insert Category.

3 Type a new category in the text box.

4 Click somewhere in your document to close the Category text box.

5 Upload your post to your blog.

HOT TIP: Once you've added some categories, they will be available from the drop-down Categories list.

HOT TIP: Try to use only one- and two-word categories that are keywords that someone might type into a search engine to find information related to your blog. If you created a blog post about tamales, you might add the categories of: food, cooking, recipes, Mexico, Mexican cooking, spicy food and tamales.

Inserting a hyperlink

The Internet would be pretty boring if it didn't include links to other places. You will probably want to use hyperlinks in your blog posts too. You can use hyperlinks to send readers to related websites and blog posts, posts within your own blog or to anywhere else you want them to go.

1 Open an existing blog post or create a new one.

2 Select a word or sentence that you want to make an active hyperlink.

3 Click the Insert tab.

4 Click Hyperlink to open the Add Hyperlink box.

5 Click Existing File or Web Page under the Link to heading on the left.

6 Type the address that you want the link to go to in the Address text bar.

7 Click OK and your hyperlink will appear in blue.

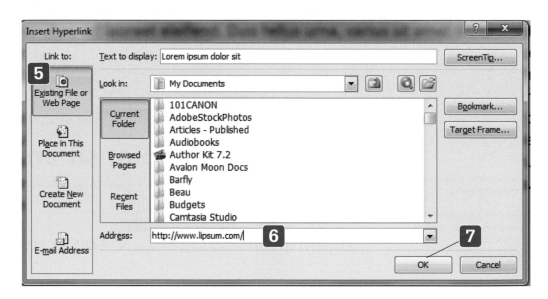

ALERT: Make sure that you use the entire web address including the http:// before the www or the link may not work properly.

? DID YOU KNOW?

The latest versions of Internet Explorer support ScreenTips. Use the ScreenTips button in the hyperlink box to add information about your link. Only Internet Explorer users will see them, however.

Following hyperlinks from within Word

You don't have to restrict the use of hyperlinks to just blog posts. You can use them in Word too. You can use hyperlinks to send readers to websites or to your blog. You can even use hyperlinks to send readers to another section of your document.

1 Open a document or create a new one that includes hyperlinks.

2 Press Ctrl on your keyboard and click the link with your mouse.

3 Wait for your web browser to open and the page to be displayed.

Lorem ipsum dolor sit amet.

Category   Languages

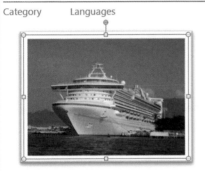

http://www.lipsum.com/
Ctrl+Click to follow link

Lorem ipsum dolor sit amet, consectetur adipiscing elit. Fusce diam velit, sollicitudin eu elementum a, sagittis a nunc. Curabitur in leo vitae est laoreet eleifend. Duis tellus urna, varius sit amet molestie at, imperdiet in nisi. Donec volutpat aliquet felis ac dignissim. Phasellus semper ligula quis dui varius eu porta purus posuere. Integer venenatis risus nec nulla rutrum tincidunt. Etiam ligula eros, suscipit a tempus sit amet, suscipit quis lorem. Praesent elit nunc, posuere sit amet suscipit vel, laoreet sit amet magna. Etiam ut rutrum ligula. Sed nisl odio, blandit non laoreet vel, lobortis a dolor. Aenean commodo porta nisl sit amet fermentum. Fusce lacinia feugiat consequat. Praesent tellus lorem, aliquet vitae vehicula sed, vehicula at lectus. Phasellus ligula eros, auctor ac ornare et, ullamcorper vel lorem. Nam at risus lacus, ut lacinia lacus. Cum sociis natoque penatibus et magnis dis parturient montes, nascetur ridiculus mus. Fusce condimentum nunc id est pulvinar suscipit. Donec rutrum ante ut tellus placerat ut dictum nibh vehicula. Praesent cursus, enim at mollis aliquam, lorem quam luctus sem, sed accumsan lacus nibh et risus.

? **DID YOU KNOW?**
If you hover your cursor over the link, the location that it leads to will be displayed.

 HOT TIP: To remove an active hyperlink from your document, right-click the link and select Remove Hyperlink. The text will remain but the clickable link will disappear.

Editing a hyperlink

What happens when you've added a hyperlink to your document or blog but you find out that the web address is no longer valid? Well, you can easily edit your existing hyperlinks to change where they lead to or what text is displayed.

1 Right-click on your hyperlink to display additional options.

2 Select Edit Hyperlink from the list.

3 Type a new address in the Address text box.

4 Type new text in the Text to Display box.

5 Click OK to update your link.

DID YOU KNOW?

You can send a reader to another location in your document by selecting Within this document from the left side of the hyperlink dialogue box.

HOT TIP: If you want your blog readers to send you email, add an email hyperlink. Once they click on it, their default email program will open with your email address in the To: field.

Inserting a photo

Not all blogs are photo blogs, but most blog posts do contain photos. It doesn't matter if they are personal photos or stock photography; pictures make your blog more interesting.

1 Open a blog post or create a new one.

2 Click the Insert tab.

3 Click Picture.

4 Browse your computer for the picture you want to add.

5 Select it with your mouse and click OK.

> ▶ **SEE ALSO:** Chapter 7: Graphics and photos

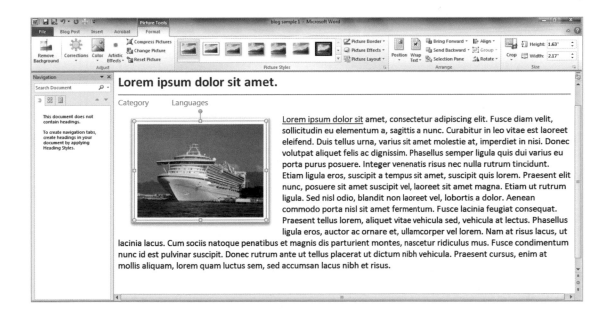

 ALERT: How your photo looks once it's uploaded is determined by what settings your blog host supports. You should check your blog to make sure it appears correctly once you've uploaded it.

 DID YOU KNOW?
When you add a photo, the Picture Tools appear. You can use these to resize and format your photo within your blog post.

Managing your blog accounts

Word 2010 gives you the option of having multiple blog accounts from a variety of blog providers. You can easily manage any number of blogs, each from a different provider if you want. Once you've added your account, you can delete it or make changes using the Manage Accounts button.

1 Click the Blog Post tab on the Ribbon.

2 Click Manage Accounts.

3 Click Add, Delete or Edit to make changes to your accounts.

4 Select a blog account and click Set As Default to make it your primary account.

5 Click Close to finish.

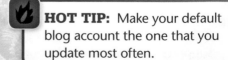

? DID YOU KNOW?
If you've made an error with your user name or password, this is where you can edit your account to reflect changes.

HOT TIP: Make your default blog account the one that you update most often.

Saving your document as a webpage

You can save your Word document as a webpage that someone can open in their browser. If you have a webhost, you can upload the page to your server and make it live on the Internet.

1 Click File on the Ribbon.

2 Click Save As.

3 Select Web Page from the drop-down Documents menu.

4 Enter a name to save your file as.

5 Select a Save location on your computer.

6 Click Save.

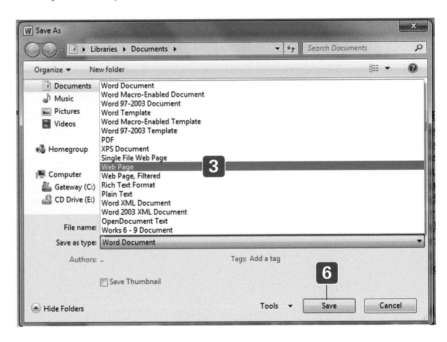

ALERT: Your formatting may appear a little differently online or some of it may not appear at all. Always double-check your page in a browser to see if there are formatting issues.

HOT TIP: Saving as a filtered webpage will reduce the size of your file, but it will also make it so you can no longer edit the document in the future.

Top 10 Problems Solved

Problem 1: Recipients are having trouble opening my documents

You're lucky enough to have the latest version of Word, but not everyone is that fortunate. Some offices, schools and home PCs are still a version or two (or three) behind. Word 2010 contains some pretty neat features that, unfortunately, just aren't compatible with previous versions. If someone has trouble opening your documents, try checking for compatibility issues and then converting them to a different file type.

1 Click File.

2 Click Info.

3 Click Check for Issues.

4 Click Check Compatibility.

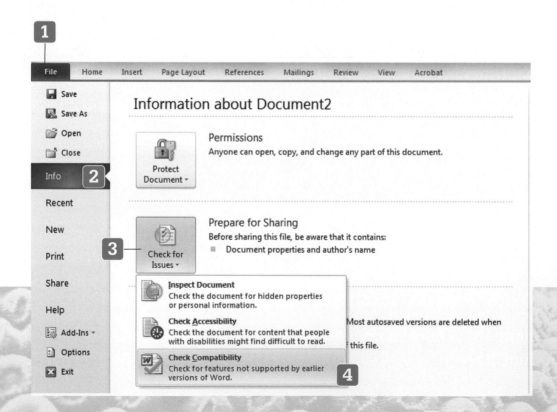

5 Review any issues that result and click OK to exit.

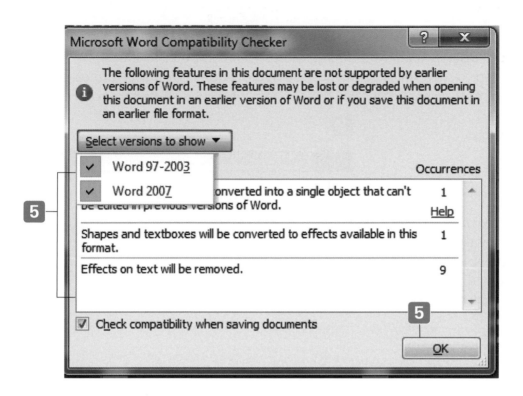

5

5

Problem 2: How do I recover lost files?

It could spell disaster if a power outage causes your computer to shut down before you managed to save your document. All that work gone! Or is it? Word can help you recover the most recent version of your file even when you haven't saved it.

1 Start Word.

2 Click File.

3 Click Recent.

4 Click Recover Unsaved Documents if your document isn't listed to the right.

HOT TIP: Make it a habit to save a copy of your document as soon as you create it; then use the Save button on the Quick Access toolbar to save frequently.

5 Select your document from the dialogue box.

6 Click OK to open it.

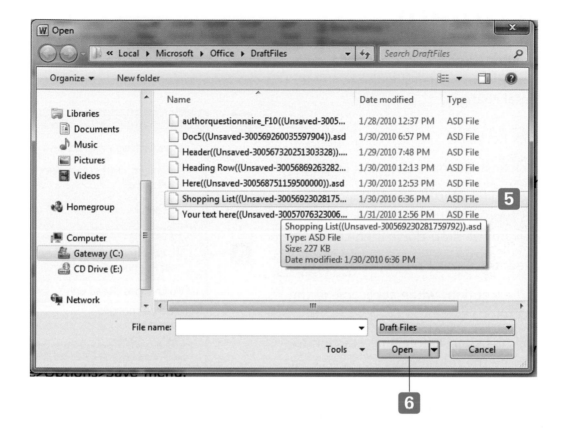

 HOT TIP: You can change how often Word saves an auto-recover version of your documents from the File>Options>Save menu.

Problem 3: I need to restrict others from changing my document

If you send documents by email frequently or otherwise share them, you can restrict other people from changing the contents. This can help prevent unauthorised or accidental changes.

1 Click Review.

2 Click Restrict Formatting and Editing.

3 Click Editing restrictions: Allow only this type of editing in the document, to activate the drop-down menu.

4 Select the type of restriction to apply.

5 Add exceptions when applicable in the Exceptions box.

6 Click Yes, Start Enforcing Protection to activate the restriction.

HOT TIP: You can also restrict formatting changes from this menu. This prevents accidental changes to your document's layout and formatting.

? DID YOU KNOW?

You can also restrict who is even allowed to open your document by using Microsoft's Information Rights Management service. You can learn more about that by clicking Restrict permission at the bottom of the Editing Restrictions menu.

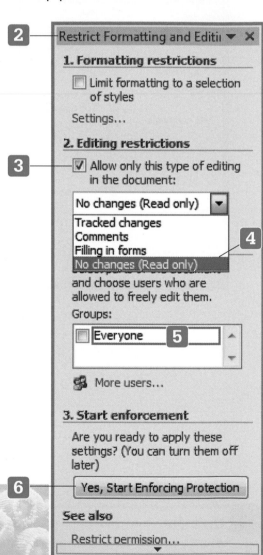

Problem 4: Unwanted symbols keep appearing in my document

Occasionally when you open a document that was created by another program, some of the characters will be replaced with symbols. Microsoft has created a compatibility pack that addresses most of the issues that caused this. More commonly the cause is that someone accidently hit the key combination to turn on Show formatting marks.

1 Click Home.

2 Click Show/Hide ¶. Continue to the next step if this doesn't resolve the issue.

3 Click File>
Option>
Display.

4 Untick any
of the boxes
under the
heading:
Always
show these
formatting
marks on
the screen.

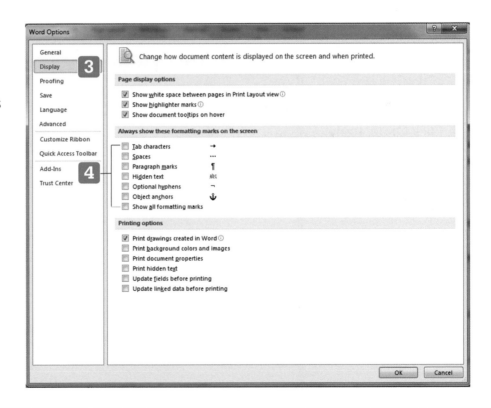

 HOT TIP: You can toggle the paragraph marks on and off with the CTRL-* shortcut (CTRL-Shift-8).

 DID YOU KNOW?

Occasionally file corruption or a virus could cause a document to display symbols. You should update your virus definitions and run a scan on your computer if the above steps do not work.

Problem 5: How can I show the Developer tab?

By default, the Developer tab is hidden. You might want to add it to your Ribbon if you plan on using pre-recorded macros, XML commands, ActiveX controls or if you want to develop programs for use within Word. You'll also need this tab to create forms and lists that people can interact with within Word.

1 Click File.

2 Click Options.

3 Click Customize Ribbon.

4 Click the tickbox next to Developer in the column to the right.

5 Click OK to apply the change and exit.

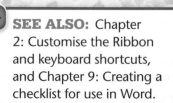

SEE ALSO: Chapter 2: Customise the Ribbon and keyboard shortcuts, and Chapter 9: Creating a checklist for use in Word.

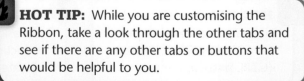

HOT TIP: While you are customising the Ribbon, take a look through the other tabs and see if there are any other tabs or buttons that would be helpful to you.

Problem 6: When pasting text I need to correct text formatting

Not all formatting can be pasted seamlessly into an existing document. Occasionally, you have to give it some help. Word gives you several Smart Paste options when pasting text from other programs or files.

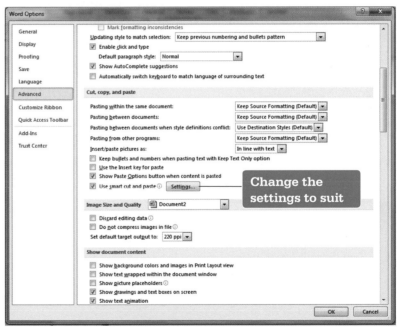

1 Cut or Copy the text that you want to paste into your document.

2 Place your insertion point where you want the pasted text to appear.

3 Click Paste from the Home tab or use CTRL-V to paste your text.

4 Click the File icon or press CTRL to view Paste options.

5 Select Keep Text Only (T) to abandon previous formatting and paste the plain text into your document.

 HOT TIP: Click Default Paste in the Paste Options menu to jump to Word's Advanced Options where you can set default paste options.

 HOT TIP: Look for the Use smart cut and paste settings button in the Advanced Options window. You can change the settings to suit your needs.

Problem 7: How do I adjust the spacing between lines and paragraphs?

If you're new to the most recent versions of Word, you might think that there is more space on your page. If so, you'd be right! In Word 2007, Microsoft increased the standard page layout, adding more space between lines and an extra line between paragraphs. If you want to select your own settings, you can.

1 Click Home.

2 Click Line and Paragraph Spacing from the Paragraph group.

3 Select the line spacing that you want.

4 Click Line and Paragraph Spacing again.

5 Click Add Space Before, or Add Space After Paragraph.

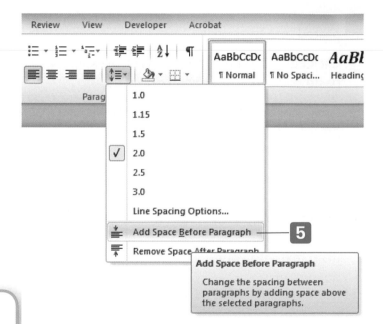

? DID YOU KNOW?
You can make single-spacing the default for all new documents. Use the Change Styles menu and select the Word 2003 Style Set.

🔥 HOT TIP: Choose a pre-assigned style from the Styles menu that has the spacing you want. Use the Live Preview function to see the changes it makes to your current spacing.

Problem 8: I want to clear my list of recent files

If you've been working in Word for a few hours, you've probably opened and closed many documents. The most recently used files are stored in the Recent section of the File tab. You can use this list to open quickly the last document you were working on. If you share your computer with others, you may want to clear the list of files that you've opened for privacy reasons.

1 Click File.

2 Click Recent.

3 Pin the documents that you want to keep on the list by clicking the push pin symbol next to the document name.

4 Right-click on a document name to access the Recent Documents menu.

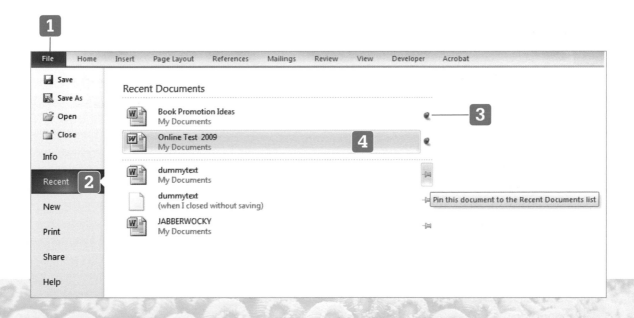

? DID YOU KNOW?

You can click the tickbox at the bottom of the Recent Files page to add previous documents to the sidebar. Tick the box and set how many documents you want to appear.

5 Select Clear unpinned items to remove the rest of the documents from the list.

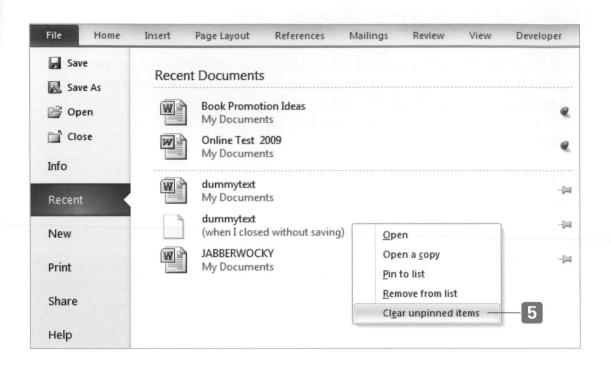

 HOT TIP: You can access AutoSave versions of your documents here, if you closed without saving them.

Problem 9: How do I install the Windows fax driver?

Several of the Office 2010 programs allow you to send files as an Internet fax. In order to use this feature, you must have the appropriate Windows drivers installed. They are not always turned on by default.

1 Click Start.

2 Click Control Panel.

3 Click Programs.

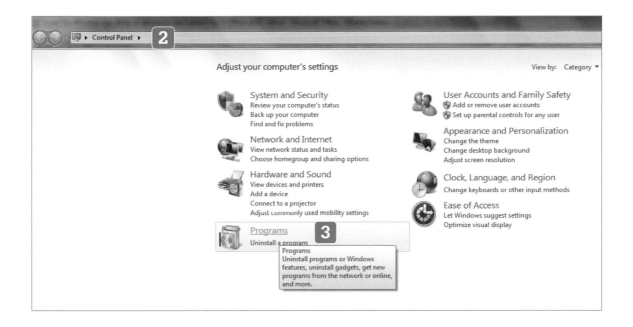

? DID YOU KNOW?

You can select Fax instead of a Printer to send your Word document as a fax.

4 Click Turn Windows features on or off under the Programs and Features heading.

5 Click Print and Document Services.

6 Click the tickbox by Windows Fax and Scan if it is not already ticked.

7 Click OK to exit.

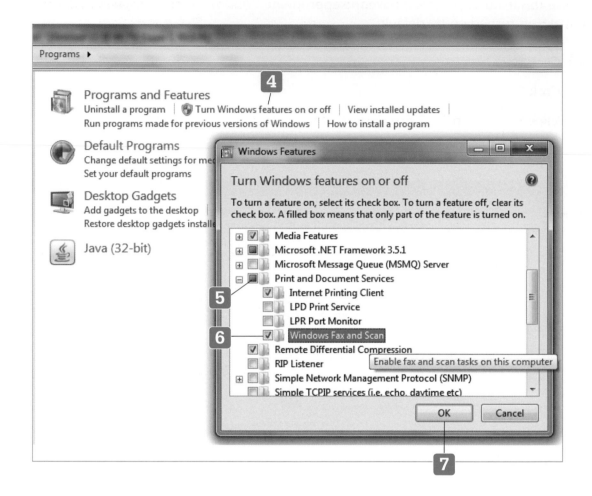

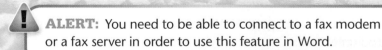

ALERT: You need to be able to connect to a fax modem or a fax server in order to use this feature in Word.

Problem 10: Where is my version number and product ID?

If you still can't find the answer that you're looking for, it might be time to ask Microsoft. If you call or use an online tech support service, the customer service representative will probably want information about your version of Microsoft Office and Word.

1 Click File.

2 Click Help.

3 View the version of Office, version of Word and your Product ID on the right.

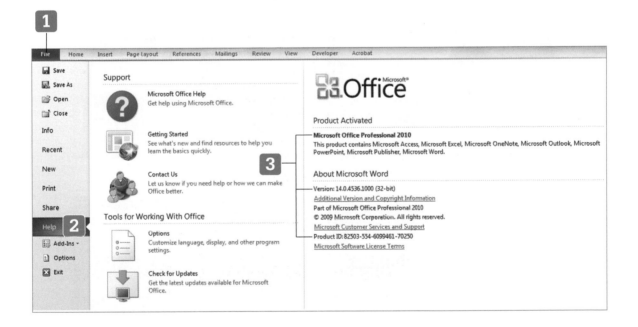

 HOT TIP: Want more detailed technical information about Word? Then click the Additional Version and Copyright Information link.

USE YOUR COMPUTER
WITH CONFIDENCE

Laptop Basics

9780273723486

Windows Vista

9780273723493

Computer Basics

9780273723479

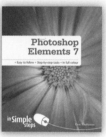
Photoshop Elements 7

9780273723523

Web Design

9780273723530

Photoshop CS4

9780273723509

Excel 2007

9780273723547

Office 2007

9780273723554

Windows 7

9780273729136

Mac Basics

9780273729297

Windows 7 FOR THE OVER 50'S

9780273729181

Laptop Basics FOR THE OVER 50'S

9780273729129

Computer Basics FOR THE OVER 50'S

9780273729174

in Simple steps

Practical. Simple. Fast.

PEARSON